THE SACRED SHE TAROT

THE SACRED SHE

TAROT

A Universal Guide to the Heart of Being

Ma Deva Padma

CREATOR OF *OSHO ZEN TAROT* & *TAO ORACLE*

ATRIA PAPERBACK
New York London Toronto Sydney New Delhi

BEYOND WORDS
Portland, Oregon

ATRIA PAPERBACK

An Imprint of Simon & Schuster, Inc.
1230 Avenue of the Americas
New York, NY 10020

BEYOND WORDS

1750 S.W. Skyline Blvd., Suite 20
Portland, Oregon 97221-2543
503-531-8700 / 503-531-8773 fax
www.beyondword.com

Managing editor: Lindsay Easterbrooks-Brown | Editors Michele Ashtiani Cohn, Bailey Potter, Carol Neiman, and Nancy Owen Barton
Copyeditor: Emmalisa Sparrow Wood | Proofreader: Kristin Thiel | Designer: Gopa & Ted2, Inc.

First Beyond Words/Atria Paperback edition November 2023

For more information about special discounts for bulk purchases, please contact Simon & Schuster Special Sales at 1-866-506-1949 or business@simonandschuster.com.

The Simon & Schuster Speakers Bureau can bring authors to your live event. For more information or to book an event, contact the Simon & Schuster Speakers Bureau at 1-866-248-3049 or visit our website at www.simonspeakers.com.

Manufactured in Hong Kong

10 9 8 7 6 5 4 3 2 1

ISBN: 978-1-58270-898-0

The corporate mission of Beyond Words Publishing, Inc.: *Inspire to Integrity*

For my beloved dancing daughter, Tika.

▼ ▼ ▼

*In deep gratitude to the spiritual lineage of mystics,
mentors, and masters whose compassionate wisdom graces
these pages and every work of art.*

CONTENTS

▼ ▼ THE CARDS ▼ ▼

SUIT OF SPIRIT

SUIT OF EARTH

SUIT OF FIRE

SUIT OF AIR

≋ SUIT OF WATER

SPECIAL ACKNOWLEDGMENTS

To the countless women who have, since the beginning of time, devoted their hearts and souls toward nurturing and bettering the world. *The Sacred She Tarot* is created in your nameless names.

To NANCY OWEN BARTON, my steadfast literary agent, editor, and soul sister. *The Sacred She Tarot* would simply not exist without your dedication and firm belief in it. We have been through so many peak-and-valley experiences as this project reincarnated many times. Finally, phoenix-like, *The Sacred She* has materialized into a work of heart we are both offering to the world.

GOPA CAMPBELL, I simply love working with you. Your expertise and calm approach to design have soothed my ruffled feathers on many occasions. Thank you for "getting me," being my safe haven, and designing with style and grace and lots of laughter.

Immense gratitude to CAROL NEIMAN for her uncanny ability to extract the essence of what I sometimes struggle to say, reconfiguring it into an approachable reading style. You are my lifetime "voice-over."

Deep thanks to MADHURI Z K AKIN for sharing your intuitive insights into the art with honesty and humor during our witchy late-night channeling sessions. Your lyrical texts brought a freshness to many of the early card interpretations that supported our proposal to find ideal publishing partners.

MICHELE ASHTIANI COHN and RICHARD COHN, your big yes to *The Sacred She Tarot* was heard all the way on the other side of the world. When we finally met, before a word was said, I felt in my bones that you were the perfect midwives for delivering this gorgeous project into the world. Like old friends reunited, I'm excited for us and all the wonderful team at Beyond Words to continue creating, playing, and working together.

To LIBBY MAGUIRE and PETER BORLAND at Atria/Simon & Schuster, a deep bow of thanks for also believing in *The Sacred She Tarot* and for joining full force with Beyond Words to help move her all around the world.

JONATHAN LYONS, thanks ever for your always-welcomed legal and publishing expertise.

ASHIKA. My heart is your heart.
You are my sacred he.

INTRODUCTION

THE SACRED SHE TAROT is the third and most personal of my tarot and oracle card offspring. Creating this body of work afforded me a precious opportunity to reflect upon my life's journey of seeking understanding and conscious awareness and then illustrating it and expressing it in words. Obviously, every person is different, yet over many years, I have found signature experiences and insights that are common to us all. With these in mind, I began the art for this deck in hopes that it would serve others in their quest for self-awareness, and in ultimately realizing the treasure of their own being.

The timing is right for *The Sacred She Tarot* to offer soulful nourishment and clarity as we transition out of an exhausted old-world order burdened under the weight of yang, or male dominance. *The Sacred She* aims to help right that imbalance by illuminating a path toward self-respect, joy, and inner peace, no matter your gender. Each of us contains both light and dark aspects. Working toward balancing these opposing forces within ourselves and in the wider world honors the wholeness of being human. Old belief systems still hold sway over every aspect of our social conditioning. By loosening the collective grip on believing that male means right, strong, and powerful, and female means weak, soft, dependent, we take a giant step toward realizing our full human potential. Each card in *The Sacred She Tarot* is created to support that end.

These cards are designed to spark recognition within yourself. They represent a range of moods, encounters, and opportunities in day-to-day life and within the dimension of spirit. Cards that feel troubling hold great potential, beckoning a deeper dive into oneself and/or the influence of external circumstances. The deck as a whole illustrates the multidimensional tapestry of individuality, as well as the conditions we face collectively.

The seventy-eight artworks comprising *The Sacred She Tarot* have arisen from observations within my own life and more broadly from the state of humanity in the twenty-first century. Our unconsciousness regarding the choices we make every day, in dealing with each other and our impact on planet Earth, has reached the tipping point. What is clear is that failing to appreciate the vital role each of us plays in a much bigger picture has created stresses and fractures within ourselves, our societies, and the entire planet.

Now is the time for us all to come to the table—to bring whatever we have to offer or simply to show up and be fully present. The *voice* speaking through this work resounds in many tongues, across oceans and continents, between peoples of every age, color, gender, nationality, and belief. Without fail, *The Sacred She* points us toward the heart of being. She is within everyone.

ABOUT THE CONTRIBUTORS

Numerous friends, mentors, and kindred spirits have generously given permission to be quoted in this book. Many are fellow travelers on the spiritual path; some I've known for nearly a half century. To me, these friendships are treasures—like seashells and wildflowers gathered over the course of this lifetime and tucked away inside my heart.

The contributors to this project are soulful partners in an expanding and much-needed realm of wisdom keepers. Their integrity, grounded empathy, and forthrightness arise from a personal commitment to apply good sense, self-reflection, and meditation to their daily lives. Some are internationally known; others are quietly doing their thing, but in every case, their compassion and generosity of spirit are not only gifts to this book but gifts to the world.

While developing *The Sacred She Tarot*, I awoke one morning with a message clearly spoken from within. It simply said, "Invite many voices to join in this work." That direction initiated an all-consuming process that began with my sending out a "Please Join Me" email to various friends, asking them to briefly respond to an artwork that was for my new tarot. Everyone was happy to play along. So one or two art images, with a few keywords for supporting direction, were sent out. Their varied responses surpassed my expectations, brought moments of hallelujah and gratitude and an upwelling of fond memories. Following each card's text in this book, the contributions from friends and luminaries appear in italics. The list of contributors at the back of the book includes a bit of information about each one.

The invitation concluded with: *My aim is for the wisdom gathered from all of us to support others in their life journey. Please, no quotes or references to old or new "masters"; there is plenty of Buddha, Osho, Rumi, etc. out in the collective. WE are a living legacy, and the time for us to speak up and share is NOW.* This exercise vividly revealed how time and distance can polish heartfelt relationships to a high shine. The message in these artworks and pages is focused on the ever-increasing need to respect each other, heal the environment, and acknowledge the feminine principle in all. My wise friend Turiya Hanover beautifully described this necessity in her reply:

Feminine power is infinitely precious—imbued with life, spirit, intuition, tenderness, and a ferocity of purpose and protection. Much of my work has been to support women, enabling them to acknowledge and trust this enigmatic presence, and to call forth age-old wisdom without fear or embarrassment or being terrified of speaking up and being seen.

Out of our receptivity arises a profound connection to spirit that is linked to the moon, cyclic changes, and to the depth and darkness of the night. It is a penetratingly psychic dimension that many of us know but keep our awareness and use of it under wraps. While in others, a nameless fear lingers in the shadows of their lives. By repressing their perception, they deny they have any connection to it at all.

Healing is a natural domain of women's work, due in large part to our intimate connection to nature, to water, to the moon, and to all that is forever changing in every moment, day by day. We contain a darkness within our wombs that is vast and mysterious, that can birth unfathomable potential. It is a true source of inner wisdom that has lived, since the beginning, in every woman, and is also alive in some men who have opened a vital connection with their female side. It is the place from which inspired creativity is born. Most artists know this fertile space and the act of entering the unknown.

The Divine Feminine can also bring an absolute sense of aloneness, an aloneness that is full of stillness and silence. In this peace our hearts sense something rising up . . . of gratitude, of prayer. And all we can do is be very calm and receptive, so we can listen to that small voice inside . . . so we can listen to Grace.

With much love,

Turiya

▼ ▼ ▼ ▼

WORKING WITH *THE SACRED SHE*

Think of *The Sacred She* not simply as a deck of cards but as having the capacity to prompt your inner voice. When appreciating it as a conduit to understanding, these vivid images compassionately direct attention back to yourself.

When treated with respect, *The Sacred She* will become a faithful friend and ally. By making a commitment to stay open-minded during your readings, you are inviting guidance from a realm of deep knowing that lies within. Develop a relationship. A great way to become intimate with *The Sacred She* is to take her to bed! Put the deck under your pillow, trusting that the dreamtime will inspire the cards' capacity to speak intuitively with authority.

I suggest that you establish a personal ritual that supports calm reflection during your sessions with

The Sacred She. Turn off your devices. Center yourself and with relaxed hands hold the cards. With closed eyes, focus your attention to summon clarity and insight. Don't rush. My personal practice is to first align my heart and mind by lightly touching the deck to the heart chakra, then to the forehead.

If you are new to tarot, I suggest you use one of the simpler spreads in the back of this book. When a specific issue is being addressed, it is helpful to write it down before proceeding. Work with an open mind to intuitively interpret what the cards express. Some people have favorite layouts while others like to experiment. There is no right or wrong way to do this.

After any session, allow space for silent reflection.

Journaling or keeping a diary of your tarot readings will help to discern patterns that can only be recognized over time.

The Sacred She Tarot consists of five suits, four of which correspond to the elements: Earth, Fire, Air, Water. The fifth suit of Spirit (known in other tarot decks as the Major Arcana) addresses spirituality, and its element is known as Ether. Each suit in this deck is designated by a color, rather than a symbol, that appears beneath the image at the bottom of the card.

The suit colors are:
Spirit—purple
Earth—green
Fire—red

Air—gray

Water—blue

The Suit of Spirit sequence begins with the card titled "0 Beginning" (the Fool in most decks), followed by twenty-one cards with Roman numerals I–XXI (1–21). The Suit of Spirit is designated by the element of Ether, which is considered spaciousness, the void that thrums with the interaction of all the other elements as they eternally mix and mingle in the dance we call existence. In human terms, it is the mystical realm of a soul's journey toward spiritual awakening.

The four other suits—Earth, Fire, Air, and Water (typically known as the Minor Arcana in other tarot decks) are numbered 1–14, with each suit opening as card number one (in other decks this card is called the Ace). There are no court cards in *The Sacred She Tarot* because all cards share equal significance. Their symbolic imagery vividly conveys meaning, with each card carrying its own weight. Cards that are commonly depicted as Pages, Knights, Queens, and Kings are simply numbered sequentially after the 10 in each suit as 11, 12, 13, 14, with the greater numbers no more important than the lesser ones.

A reference key appears on the bottom of the card texts that correlates to equivalent cards from two classic tarots. Unknown to most, these tarot decks were channeled and illustrated by women whose names were unacknowledged for many years. Without the devotion and significant talents of Pamela

Colman Smith and Lady Frieda Harris, the *Rider-Waite* and *Crowley Thoth* tarot decks would simply not exist.

Pamela "Pixie" Colman Smith was commissioned by Arthur Waite, a member of the Hermetic Order of the Golden Dawn, to illustrate his concept of tarot, which is now arguably the most recognized deck in the world. The result was the *Waite-Smith Tarot* that soon after was renamed *Rider-Waite Tarot*, bypassing Smith altogether, while acknowledging William Rider, the publisher, instead. *The Sacred She Tarot*, in deference to Smith's exceptional creation, will honor her deck in the reference key with the initials **RWS**, for *Rider-Waite-Smith*.

The second woman to be honored is Lady Frieda Harris, whose paintings were created for the *The Book of Thoth* by Aleister Crowley. Her artworks were later reproduced as Crowley's *Thoth Tarot*. Lady Frieda was a disciple of Crowley, who taught her divination, introduced her to the *I Ching*, and described her as a devoted genius. In regard to their collaboration, she insisted on her own anonymity out of deference to him. Lady Frieda Harris died in India in 1962. Neither she nor Crowley lived to see her art produced as a tarot. In honoring her exemplary creation, **H** for *Harris* will follow **TH** for *Thoth* and will appear on these pages as **THH**.

SUIT of SPIRIT is designated by the color purple at the bottom of each card. This suit contains the spiritual keys to the development of human consciousness and is traditionally known as the Major Arcana. In *The Sacred She Tarot*, this suit begins with a card titled "0 Beginning" that is followed by Roman numerals I–XXI (1–21).

SUIT of EARTH is designated by the color green at the bottom of each card. It is the suit of physicality, materialism, and the environment and is traditionally known as the suit of pentacles. In some decks it is depicted as discs, coins, shields, rainbows, and so forth.

SUIT of FIRE is designated by the color red at the bottom of each card. It is the suit of dynamic movement and energy and is traditionally known as the suit of wands. In some decks it is depicted as clubs, lightning, spells, and so forth.

SUIT of AIR is designated by the color gray at the bottom of each card. It is the suit of intellect, reasoning, and conduct and is traditionally known as the suit of swords. In some decks it is depicted as arrows, clouds, challenges, and so forth.

SUIT of WATER is designated by the color blue at the bottom of each card. This is the suit of sensitivities, emotions, and relationships and is traditionally known as the suit of cups. In some decks it is also known as chalices, bowls, hearts, and so forth.

▾ ▾ SPIRIT ▾ ▾

*Suit of consciousness, spiritual evolution,
contemplation, transformation, karma, and wisdom,
commonly known as the Major Arcana.*

⠂⠂ O ⠂⠂
BEGINNING

BEGINNING INITIATES A VIBRANT JOURNEY of transformation that requires openness and a mighty leap of faith. Fueled by a longing to grow and experience, she trusts in existence to guide her flight into the unknown. She will find that whether active or still, progressing or retreating, gaining or losing, she is a unique expression of the source. This solo flight commences an inner revolution that in the highest sense activates consciousness and compassion.

Stimulated by the promise of a fresh start, this precious

being embodies the hope that is our human nature. Her flight is a passage revealing many and varied situations that will change her psychologically, emotionally, and physically. As her old behavior patterns fade, she realizes the expansive liberation of her inborn potential.

The Sacred She Tarot is created to encourage your innate abilities, sharpen your instincts, and welcome the inner peace lying dormant within you. May this fresh beginning encourage the recognition that you are and have always been a child of wonder.

The timeless wisdom contained here confirms that as one door closes, another opens. All is flow; life never stands still. In every moment is a beginning. Feel the uplift and your beating heart. The dawning that is *now* awaits your flight. You are carried. You are welcomed.

Come with me.
You are me.
We cannot separated be.
This journey is both yours and mine.
May we rise and soar outside of time.
With every breath that we are taking,
so goes the world that is our making.

·· I ··
ALCHEMY

THE ALCHEMIST STANDS POISED, ready for action, and balanced within the cardinal elements at the intersection of heaven and earth. She is an innovative conduit who works with the forces of nature. Her aim is to understand the fundamentals of things and to use that knowledge to effect positive change.

This transformer takes full advantage of the essential tools that are available to her now. The sword keeps her to the point and cuts through the tangential. She draws strength and inspiration from fire yet remains fully grounded on the earth. The waters of life cleanse and restore her. Her companion, the farsighted eagle, provides overview while guiding her toward self-realization.

Working in tune with natural cycles requires patience and trust, as well as resilience. It does not call for shortcuts or pulling strings to impress. Utilize the eagle's intense focus to further your transformative work. Soar on the winds of change and seek out whatever is needed to sharpen your wits and your vision.

Inner alchemy is a transformative process that employs the combined energies of body, mind, and spirit to open awareness, refine sensitivity, and develop meaningful purpose in one's life. It is a passage, and a returning, that requires forgiveness, responsiveness, and devotion to transmute the mud of ignorance into the lotus flower of consciousness.

Sometimes I swim in muddy water,
no crystal-clear mountain streams.
But in that muddy water I find the elements.
The sharp tang of copper.
The keen iron taste deep within these bones.
The crystalline deposits of loss. The bedrock of shame.
And from this pure Divine Alchemy there arises
the true possibility
to awaken from old dreams.

THE UNKNOWABLE

ENIGMATIC, SHROUDED, THIS PRESENCE rests atop a crescent moon, floating between the known and unknown worlds. As the guardian of secrets and psychic forces, she has heard all the questions that humanity has ever asked . . . yet she's far too wise to trivialize their queries with answers. Cloaked in an impenetrable veil of mystery, her authority embodies the riddle of life that can never be explained or fully grasped. The crescent moons crowning her denote timeless intuitive understanding that emanates from deep within the subconscious.

Any answers you have been hoping for will not be given now. Surrender the need to know and gently relax back into yourself. Become open to the source of your longing. Intellect alone is incapable of grasping the full scope of the present; its nature is too immense, inscrutable.

When encountering the unknown, remember that existence is unfathomably vast, mysterious, and baffling to the inquisitive mind. Accept this opportunity to let go and let be. In most tarot decks, this card is known as the High Priestess. She is universally acknowledged as a threshold, the gatekeeper of secrets who bestows understanding only when the seeker is receptive. No action is required. Rather, this is a time for silent inactivity. Life is buoyant and moving, even when it feels like it's standing still.

Only when we dare to be alone, with attention turned inward, can we fully trust this deepest intuition and wisdom. When we stop pleasing everybody, when we stop wanting to be like everybody, when we stop striving to be perfect, or to find a partner . . . then this intimate dimension opens her wings and rains all blessings upon us.

·· III ··
MOTHER NATURE

MOTHER NATURE'S CREATION is limitless and inconceivably diverse. No administration or bureaucracy is needed for her to modify the overall pattern to support equilibrium. She breathes life into every aspect of her magnificent conception. From humans to viruses, all serve life's purpose to propagate, grow, evolve. It is natural. Our shared home, this Earth, is her inspiration. Here, all elements merge and mingle in an elegant balance of the finely tuned ecosystems that we know as the web of life. Having long believed ourselves to be the planet's most intelligent life form, we've failed to appreciate that we are but a tiny part of her cosmic creation.

The idea of taming or conquering nature exposes our hubris and immaturity that has tipped her delicate balance into troubling territory. By invoking her remedy, we face extreme upheaval, as she heals the damage done by our foolishness. To the extent we've abused the natural order, the more demanding is our task to correct it. This applies as much to our personal relationships as it does to the environment.

Treat these challenges as opportunities for learning and healing. Figure out how to nurture nature. Take responsibility for the choices you make in supporting the exquisite intelligence of the natural world. Mother Nature always has the last word.

Low tide! The glory of gathering medicinal seaweeds in the earliest morning light.
Behold, the magnificence! The Herbs of the Sea, swirling, dancing at my feet . . . a starfish!
Untold beauty engulfs me. Now, I am encircled in yellow brilliance, a field of flowering Saint John's wort.
I imbibe its offering of solace, calm, safety, peace.
Yes. I am uplifted, just sitting here, in deepest reverence for her creation.

·· IV ··
ORDER

YOU COULD SAY that each of us is a living, breathing mandala. Whatever your imaginings, hopes, dreams, or plans, all radiate from a center that is you. It is the same in nature, from spiraling galaxies to the formation of an embryo. Without a source, nothing happens. No outer or inner life, only stasis.

This card acknowledges the grand design that is at the heart of existence, the fulcrum around which everything transpires. We search for meaning in life, to understand the incomprehensible mysteries that exist within us and in the cosmos. By looking into the basic tenets that govern the natural world, we see they are the same within us, in a butterfly, and in the life of a buddha.

Growth starts from a single point, marking the ground from which our projects, relationships, and creations come into being. To manifest anything, we must plant a seed.

Make a plan. Chart your course with plenty of flexibility to adapt to the stresses of change. Many meditations focus on bringing the myriad of thoughts to a still point where there is clarity and calm. That point is where a strong foundation can be formed; if it arises from the center of being, its integrity will hold.

Nature unfolds effortlessly. Not only as patterns and form but also as the flow and expansion of space— a vast and fluid living cosmos. There is a "rightness," an effortless effort at play that we recognize as the harmony of inner and outer nature in our lives. It is here in this spontaneous order that we find beauty in the chaos, fullness in the emptiness, and consciousness abiding in the mystery.

·· V ··
WISDOM KEEPER

A WISDOM KEEPER'S INTELLIGENCE is never found in a book. It results and grows from respecting and accepting every aspect of their life experience. Wisdom Keepers see signs and cycles in their surroundings, wherever they call home. Presence and place conjoin in an intimate dialogue that they learn from, every day.

Eagle-eyed observers, these teachers offer their understanding freely and without pretension—over a cup of some earthy brew or while walking in nature. The informality of such exchanges belies their profound depth of insight. For one who is open and receptive, the exchange can be powerful enough to prompt a breakthrough that resets a viewpoint or life direction. It may take years before the full impact of an exchange with a keeper of wisdom is assimilated.

Rational thought is useless when learning from one who walks the path of self-knowledge. They live their truth while sharing their vision with whomever seeks them out. They are like a well in the desert for those who thirst for wisdom.

The quality of time spent with a Wisdom Keeper is intense yet light, infused with a mix of compassion, generosity, patience . . . and much humor.

Over decades, the frozen effects of trauma melted, opening my heart to receive the guidance of wisdom, precisely when I needed it the most. It was as if existence stepped in and whispered, "Listen." Once, while struggling with issues of personal power and acceptance, I spotted a quote that is still shared with the women I mentor: "I would rather be hated for who I am than loved for who I am not." Wisdom is always available when you stay available.

·· VI ··
LOVE

LOVE IS LOVE. Love is not this:

Love is not complicated or cruel. Love is not blind or dumb. Love is not abusive. Love is not demanding or controlling. Love is not a test or a problem. Love is not political, greedy, or stingy. Love is not possessive, impatient, or wishy-washy. Love wants not, needs not. Love holds no grudge, stakes no claim, has no boundary, no face, no gender, color, or creed.

Just as sunlight dances over water or silently enters a darkened room, illuminating all that it touches, so does love gently glow from within, brightening all. Love's radiance loses nothing, yet the more it is felt, the more it increases. The wellspring of love never runs dry. Just as a solitary flame is undimmed by lighting a thousand candles, each of us is a conduit for love. In that way, we can illuminate, nourish, and support the world.

Union may be symbolized by two wax candles, the tips of which touch each other so closely that there is but one light; or again, the wick, the wax, and the light become one, but the one candle can again be separated from the other, and the two candles remain distinct . . . But spiritual marriage is like rain falling from heaven into a river or stream, becoming one and the same liquid, so that the river and rainwater cannot be divided; or it resembles a streamlet flowing into the ocean, which cannot afterward be disunited from it. This marriage may also be likened to a room into which a bright light enters through two windows—though divided when it enters, the light becomes one and the same.

·· VII ··
TURNING POINT

THE TURNING POINT represents a quantum shift that brings clarity by revealing what just moments before was held up by uncertainty, confusion, and doubt. From this point, you are released from the exhausting need to have all the answers.

Don't waste the inspiration gained at this supportive time by retreating into an old mindset that has kept you wandering in the dark until now. This dramatic shift of energies is as natural as winter's contraction evolving into the colorful expansiveness of spring.

As tensions subside, you'll feel uplifted, as though returning home after a long absence. Enjoy this boost in confidence but take care to not waste its support. Use this turning point to strengthen yourself while expanding your horizons. There is so much more to be discovered.

It is natural to sometimes find ourselves deep within the woods, the bounds of our minds, where we cannot see beyond its darkness and confusion. What is the next step? At this vulnerable point, we are disconnected from our inner navigation and feel lost in ourselves, not knowing what we need. After failing to find a way through, something beautiful and very human occurs. In that fraction of a moment comes a turning point when something shifts, breaking the spell. You look up and see a crack of light between trees, drawing you to the opening at forest's edge—to where everything that seemed enclosed, impossible, now becomes possible.

It is at this moment you are compelled to move—beyond the limitations of the mind. You are in transition from the old to the new. Something has changed. The turning point has arrived.

· VIII ·
COMPASSION

THIS FEARSOME DENIZEN from the primordial depths symbolizes our shadow side—the untamed aspect of our nature we are taught to suppress. Yet childlike innocence embraces the menacing entity with kindness and full acceptance, as it would a long-lost friend.

By acknowledging this unnerving characteristic of our own nature, it is reassured and calmed, becoming a supportive ally rather than one that wreaks havoc. When the murky fear of uncertainty and trusting openness merge, their union produces compassion. Without the mud, there can be no flowering. This card epitomizes the result of an inner alchemy that occurs when our radiant inner child and dreaded elemental nature finally work in tandem. Coaxing the shadow self toward consciousness requires calm determination, open-mindedness, humility, and patience. As shocking passions from the past surface, they must be acknowledged and explored with honesty, unwavering integrity, acceptance, and ultimately, forgiveness. Once we stop condemning and suppressing our awkward, uncouth traits, they finally transform into tolerance and empathy. Greeting this resident from your inner swamp can be a profound reunion that creates wholeness and is the key to transformation.

not a shadow crosses this child's face
the dragon in its ancient lair has yet to stir
but if her gifts and life conspire, if hearth can hold the fire
she will survive the storm, the flapping of great wings
and come to know in herself, in her friends, in all people
the prehistory of this our body, and delight in it
the boundless heart, our source of strength
and creativity,
find, suddenly appearing, a great love for those
who walk these roads
and swim these waters—for all things born of earth

⁘ IX ⁘
SOLITUDE

THE SEEKER TURNS AWAY from life's occupations and passes through a portal into an introspective world. Her quest for understanding requires that she assume a newfound solemnity. Instead of jostling life's demands, she responds to an instinctive urge to withdraw from day-to-day affairs for a time and face herself completely. Her vivid cloak, woven from a lifetime of experience, will change. She cannot yet know that one day, when she returns to the busy marketplace world, quietude will have bestowed upon her brilliant rainbow hues of understanding, revealed from the inside out.

What does retreat from daily life entail? A response to a deep longing to open into the unexplored landscape of oneself. The call is as clear as a finger pointing at the moon.

In meditation and mindfulness practices, looking inward restores a spacious connection to the essence of all. So many methods are available for calming the mind. For some, the urge to experience inner peace is so strong that they will withdraw from the company of others entirely. For others, it may mean a sojourn to further their spiritual practice.

Once the inner voice calls for a period of solitude, heed the message. Your life will be profoundly enriched by it.

There's a solitary watchtower where the sky swamps you, flushes out the ragged flotsam of stale thought.
Up there above the treetops, the watcher finds a yes to being herself—with her Self. She is alone;
she is not lonely. The clear air offers clean-washed colors, delights of unheard music, and the
spacious formlessness of beauty, love, and truth. This solitude is freedom: freedom
to prospect, explore, enrich, and incline us to who we really are.

X
CHANGE

THE PROSPECT OF LIFE CHANGES can freak us out. We go to psychics, mediums, card readers, and astrologers to predict and safeguard against the future. Yet change is the constant we all share and must live with. Our every breath is its harbinger.

If your self-confidence solely depends on the constancy of your environment, your relationships, your body, then you are depending on a soap bubble. Denial of life's changing nature is like living in a sandcastle that requires constant shoring up against the certainty of an incoming tide. Whether living in a penthouse, a yurt, or a shack, we are all subject to forces beyond our control that can leave heartbreak, chaos, and insecurity in their wake.

Accepting the inevitability of change heightens the awareness of life as transitory. This inclusive perspective values the present in a totally new light, revealing *this moment* as where life is actually happening. When the unknown "next" is no longer projected as a problem, a mindful response, rather than a fearful reaction, becomes possible. Accepting change as the way existence constantly transforms itself helps to bring us into the fullness of now.

We're all in the midst of sweeping global and personal changes, and our options are clear: stubbornly attempt to replicate the good ole days or face reality as it is and quantum leap into unexplored territory.

One of the ways I divert from the real possibility of a contraction into fear is to feel the ways in which I am not alone. We are all here tottering on the edge, consciously or not. We are dangling, hanging, grasping, swinging, and sometimes just letting go.

ᵛᵛ XI ᵛᵛ
BALANCING

BALANCE IS NOT A STABLE, STEADFAST STATE. Its changing nature adjusts, refines, and reveals a living dance that affects all of life and our planet, whether we're aware of it or not.

Imbalance arises from inclining too far in a certain direction. If you're wondering how to support equilibrium, relax and reconnect with your center, which is calm and neutral. Whether a bias is to the right or left—helpful or debilitating—by becoming one-sided, impartiality and stability are lost. Yet even in the most extreme situations, over time, balance can be restored.

Weigh the effects of your opinions and tendencies and observe the scope of their impact. We're not only responsible for managing our own health—we're also responsible for monitoring the changing conditions on Earth. When our outlook is on behalf of ourselves, tomorrow's children, and our planet, restorative conditions and practices follow.

Balancing is a constant adjustment to dynamic changes in the inner and outer environments. The body is an organism that searches for homeostasis, for a neutral that allows rest. That search requires movement, adjustment, continual change. In restful moments, we feel peace, equanimity, and ease. Meditation and contemplation support that calm state while opening us to connect with the preciousness of existence and our sacred nature.

In the balancing between extremes, similarities and differences, the yin and yang in all, nature reveals an ever-flowing life force within every living cell.

By respecting the dynamics of balance, we can weather anything life throws at us. We lose balance and find it again. We lose connection to Self and find it again. Balancing is an innate expression of health.

·· XII ··
WAKING UP

AN UNCOMFORTABLE TIME OF CHANGE turns the familiar world upside down. Imagine the disorientation of this iconic creature of the night when something shakes her awake at midday—unaccustomed brightness, dazed and confused, no clue what has just happened. You and this bat have much in common. For a little while you both should expect to be a little wobbly! There is no need to rush and try to put things back together. If you can't find your feet, wait while your inner axis adjusts.

In some cultures, bats symbolize rebirth, while to the Mesoamerican tribes, they portend a time of surrendering to one's fate, to one's destiny. Over the course of a lifetime, we experience out-of-the-blue events that jolt us awake, exposing unexpected aspects of the present. Later, this phase will be remembered as an eye-opening period of transformation.

Despite any insecurity you may be feeling now, know that existence is supporting your awakening consciousness. You have earned this. Welcome to a brand-new perspective and a renewed you.

Waking up means remembering to be fully alive, in every breath and the spaces in between.
For flying foxes, night is day and day is night; they live upside down as others live upright. And although
bats seed our forests and pollinate flowers, they are regarded as pests. To the crowd, anyone that challenges
the status quo is misunderstood, an outsider, troubling. With opened eyes and increased perception,
be undaunted now, guided with a crystal clarity even in darkness.

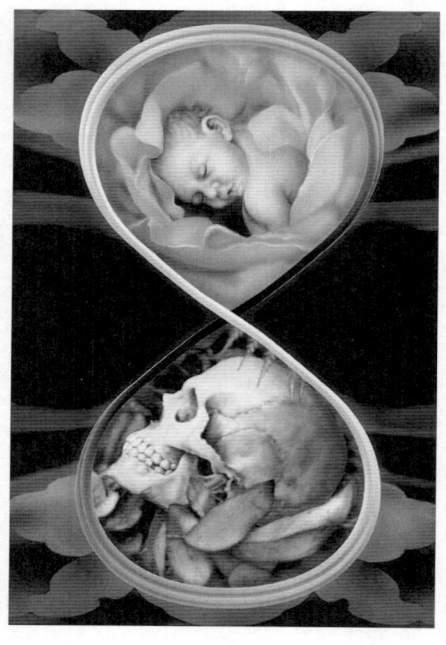

·· XIII ··
TRANSITIONING

THE SACRED CYCLE of birth, life, death, and birth again is eternally recurring. Every new life is a fresh beginning, a journey with its potential yet to be realized. Death is another passage that we recognize as a departure into some mysterious unknown. At both points of transition from one world to another, everything changes; the familiar is totally left behind.

If birth and death are viewed from the perspective that nothing is ever lost, then we can see that existence is always in the process of weaving every particle into a vast and interconnected celestial body. There is a marvelous ribboning, eternally connecting everyone and everything beyond the confines of time and space.

In our own lifetime, many actual and metaphorical deaths, births, and rebirths occur as the old makes way for the new. Every fresh start plays a vital role in the great cycling of existence as it interlaces expansion and closure, filling and emptying.

On a personal level, when subtle signals of an inner revolution arise, the outcome is unknown and even unknowable. A sea change is imminent that could manifest in any area of your life. By loving yourself through this transition, in fear and in joy, you'll be utterly transformed. And you will know that every aspect of your journey so far was essential for this rebirth to happen.

Birth and Death
A Portal
To Infinity and Timelessness
Here and Now
In this Moment . . . Ahh!!!

WHAT TO SAY ABOUT KARMA? When funky, it seems to arise from foolish unawareness that repeats the same old patterns. When good, it is taken as a happy payoff for some good deed in the past. Survey yourself to understand what generates harmony and well-being or discord and pain. What is missing? Perhaps it is your presence, full acceptance of your totality, whole and complete.

Imagine that each of us is a unique melody, the sound of which resonates from whatever we think and do. Remember, every moment offers a choice of whether to venerate life or denigrate it. It is your choice; there is no doctrine, no right or wrong way to be, other than to unconditionally hold what is.

Think of karma as cause and effect, truth or consequences. Consciousness is as valid as unconsciousness; they are the day and the night. There is no better or worse, only *what is*. Cruelty produces suffering that furthers cruelty. Kindness creates feel-good vibes that spread like ripples in a pond.

Without evaluating yourself as bad or good, simply observe how your viewpoint determines your feelings and outlook. Freedom from the confines of your judgments opens the way for living wholeheartedly. Be the person who can change your world—there is no need for apologies or beliefs.

Karma, for me, is an ache in my heart and being, when I remember the said or done things
that have unconsciously hurt others, and myself. I cannot change the past . . .
Karma is also the amazing gratefulness, light, and connection I feel for all the beauty
that surrounds me and all that I have been given in this lifetime.

·· XV ··
REPRESSION

MANY OF US HAVE BEEN TAUGHT from childhood that anger is bad and expressing it improper. "Life isn't fair," we're told. "That's just the way it is." We should just suck it up and move on. So when anger or a sense of injustice arises, we stuff it down, repress it. Often, we condemn and blame ourselves for having those horrible feelings in the first place.

However, it's precisely our untamed, fierce nature that empowers our capacity to endure against all odds by expressing an intense focus or response that doesn't back down when confronted. Anger festers when repressed. Then gnawing discomfort rises from our "unacceptable" thoughts and feelings that need to escape the tight lid we've kept on them.

This image encourages you to unearth and befriend the unruly, visceral aspect of your nature.

Living in fear of this quality keeps you fragmented, afraid to stand up for yourself and set yourself free. This inner alchemy transforms damaged goods into treasure. Acknowledging the good, the bad, and the ugly unshackles the power of your wild and primitive heart and transforms fear into courage.

One of the most difficult and yet most empowering things I have experienced was coming face-to-face with my own self-hatred. That recognition exposed the extent of my efforts to hide all that was considered "wrong" in me—by my family, school, church, society at large. The belief that some flaw within me ran so deep that my very survival depended upon burying the shame of it in the "darkness" of my unconscious. Weakness, fearfulness, rage, terrible cravings . . . in repressing them, I was petrifying my body, freezing my emotions in stubborn self-righteousness.

·▾ XVI ·▾
CRISIS

RISIS JOLTS US INTO THE PRESENT. Our prior reality is gone—gone for good—and we're left with raw pain, vulnerabilities and untested strengths exposed. Horrific mass events of earthquakes, floods, plagues, and war decimate our sense of place and purpose. Torn from focusing solely on ourselves and close ones, our awareness of the bigger picture, shared with so many, dramatically intensifies.

Personal crises can be just as earthshaking, forcing us to face uninvited, sweeping change. It is wrenching when dreams are shattered and relationships that once meant everything are gone. Losing what you have counted on to support or inspire your life impels you to re-evaluate everything. Yet, calamities can inspire and empower positive change.

We grow wise not from being comfortable but from being nudged, shaken, and jolted awake, to see that life can sometimes be most supportive when it utterly wrecks our dreams. Crisis humbles us by bringing us to our knees, yielding to forces we suddenly realize have never really been in our hands.

We are all players in the unpredictable narrative of existence. After the storm clears and tears have dried, you will value each day more than you ever thought possible. Then, what was feared is understood as a shock that shattered illusions, awakening you to a new reality.

Life always manages to present situations that throw us off balance. Weathering critical events depends upon the ability to respond with equanimity rather than react out of habit or fear. Becoming aware of our impulsive reactions makes space for acceptance of what is. In this way, the belief that balance depends upon the "rightness" of the external disappears in the light of self-awareness.

·· XVII ··
UNDERSTANDING

AFTER CRISIS AND UPHEAVAL, a silence of understanding arises. It is an intensely personal experience of expanded insight into oneself and still deeper into the vast mystery of life. This deliverance is a state of grace. One is still . . . and knows.

Our senses are the window to the soul, and it is within the soul that the alchemy of understanding occurs.

True understanding is beyond language and beyond words.

While it is owned by none, it can be shared by all. It is universal. Words are the tools of understanding, but silence offers our inmost understanding that resonates gently from the heart of being.

Like a smile, it cannot be borrowed; it can only be expressed.

Understanding grows through self-awareness, reflection, and witnessing whatever life brings . . . the pain, the challenges, the attachments, and the joy. Don't turn away from the trials and hardships of life, for they cultivate understanding that calms the mind and brings peace to the heart.

Profound understanding can occur in a moment when a fragment of insight clarifies a life lesson, even after many lifetimes. In the right timing of things, while watching an everyday event like a leaf falling, an illuminating shift in perception occurs that reveals the extraordinary in the ordinary. Understanding can be elusive, hovering in the mist, just out of reach, until, when forged by the practice of witnessing and meditation, it rises to the surface of one's consciousness.

When guided by good judgment, understanding becomes wisdom. Understanding and wisdom are soul mates, for without understanding, there can be no wisdom, and without wisdom, understanding loses its purpose. Together they shine a light on one's path ahead.

ANXIETY

WHENEVER WE ARE BLINDED to the obvious, choosing instead to believe in conjured-up narratives, we trick ourselves like Wile E. Coyote does. Fascination with his own cleverness keeps him perpetually distracted, and so he repeatedly trips over his own tail and commits the same mistakes—traps himself, appears foolish, reckless, laughable.

By taking ourselves, our beliefs, and our opinions too seriously, we become hypnotized by the brilliance of our imagined reality. Dreamed-up fictions spawn fearfulness that can degenerate into paranoia, devastating the quality of life. Looking into the roots of our fears and anxiety takes courage. By refusing to admit to the pain we feel, which often is rooted in the long-ago past, we stay trapped in the strangle hold of dread.

Answering these may be helpful: What are you refusing to accept or longing to communicate?

Is there something hidden within your distress that might reveal what is keeping it going?

Is it *really* anxiety that hurts, or is it your reluctance to depart from the cozy security of trumped-up fantasies, imagined storylines, paranoid projections?

I am a coyote, lurking in the shadows, frightened by the light but drawn by the heat. Wanting to be warmed but not burned, filled but not consumed.

I struggle because that's what minds do, whipsawed by hope and fear. I fight to preserve a life I despise. The alternative being so vast.

If I could find some basis, some viewpoint, some foundation that could not be doubted, would it give me peace, like a lily pad for a frog or a burrow for a hare?

Somehow it seems more honest to talk about my troubles than the gentle song of waves, shimmering in moonlight, lapping on the shore.

·· XIX ··
JOY

W HENEVER JOY ARRIVES on the scene, the world unexpectedly brightens. Joyfulness bubbles up with no fanfare, no formal invitation, no calendar reminder, just simply hopping, skipping, or soaring in full flight. When joy wafts in, the air is refreshed, life fills with promise, and the serious mind loosens its grip.

The innocence of children channels joy spontaneously, effortlessly. But joy is available to everyone, regardless of age or infirmity. Joy's appearance comes bearing gifts that can open closed hearts and release any tightfisted point of view with ease. Each of us is different, yet we are the same when it comes to experiencing the sweet pleasures of joy. How immensely versatile she is—expressed in infinite ways throughout the natural world.

Never worry about joy being too much, inappropriate, running out, not following protocols—because joy is free and limitless. Her manner may tickle and nudge. She can appear out of the blue, in any shape or size, and even smile invisibly within the heart.

Put the welcome mat out for joy, and once she appears, don't hesitate. Swing the door wide open.

Joy's arrival can quicken our affections and give wings to our fondest dreams.

Joy

We often miss her because we were looking for
something dramatic and huge.
But it turns out joy is quiet and tiny—as tiny as
a sliver of light, small enough
to slip through the cracks of a broken heart or the
splintered planks of a capsized dream.

Joy's only purpose is to pour herself into us so that
we might beam her around
to those who thirst for light. She asks that we keep
her secret in our hearts.

⋎⋎ XX ⋎⋎
LIBERATION

W E BECOME ACCUSTOMED TO OUR PATTERNS
of living, accepting them as normal—but a time
comes when we see that those old patterns and
habits are keeping us caged. Once the light of this understanding switches on, we experience a first glimpse of spaciousness
beyond the world we know. Then a profound longing arises
within; the heart uplifts, and we are no longer afraid of step-
ping out into the unknown.

When the deep-rooted longing for change arises, a mighty leap of faith is required—and there is no turning back. In nature, this awesome rite of passage plays out in the breathtaking transition from nest to full flight. Only when ready, with great heart and wings spread wide, does a fledgling soar into the vast, empty sky.

Liberation marks a period of sweeping change that is both fundamental and absolute. The freedom addressed here involves a quickening that thrums from deep within and cannot be ignored. Be gentle with yourself and others while undergoing this transformation; it is nothing less than a liberating expansion of consciousness.

No matter how intense or unacceptable our feelings are, it is so important to welcome them, allow them to be present in the body and in the heart. In that welcome, each feeling is a portal to a dimension of our essential nature, to peace, and to true freedom.

We all long for freedom, yet we often deny our human reality. We think we should be above it all. Here we allow ourselves to be in our feelings, welcome and accept them as a doorway to our human nature and essence.

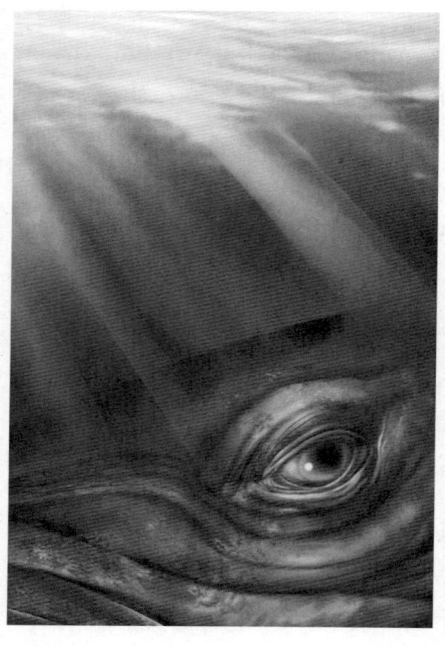

WISDOM

WHALES HAVE AN INTELLIGENCE far greater than we comprehend. Their massive bodies and complex brains carry a consciousness that cultures from prehistory to the present have respected as holding knowledge of life's beginning.

Those mythologies, songs, and stories enrich us with timeless essential truths about coming up for air and diving deep—to survive, reflect, and mature. Whales are long-lived, learning and developing deep below the ocean's surface. As mammals, they are much like us. However, as ocean dwellers, their air dependence demands cyclic surfacing.

Breakthroughs require energy that, with intention, can be transformative. When a growth cycle comes full circle, a fresh cycle begins. Within that spiraling pattern there is a point of transition— think of whales breaching the boundaries of water and air. Their very being depends on it. For humans with a conscious intention, life's in-between phases are meaningful opportunities for reflection that open the inner eye of awareness. Insight (observing within) and overview (observing from above) are vital for activating the empathic understanding that results in wisdom.

However stormy the seas of your life may be, diving beneath the roiling surface into a calm inner dimension, where nothing is expected of you, will provide relaxed space for reflection. With the benefit of cool, buoyant detachment, review the choices you've made and their outcomes. Let go of anything that fails to support your well-being or denies you the freedom to express your fullest potential.

After numerous breaches and breakthroughs, a soulful understanding surfaces in the name of wisdom.

I want to age like sea glass. I want to enjoy the journey and let my preciousness be, not in spite of the impacts of life, but because of them.

▼ ▼ EARTH ▼ ▼

*Suit of nature, physicality, reliability,
work, the world, materialism, and commerce,
commonly known as the suit of pentacles or coins.*

·· 1 ··
ROOTS

UNIMAGINABLY ANCIENT, the roots of life reach back into the very origins of our planet and the universe itself. We are supported and nourished by vast underlayers of mitochondrial connectivity and soil made rich through ever-cycling eons of birth, growth, and decay.

Buried treasure is contained within these roots that empowers self-awareness. Knowledge, gained by unearthing the origins of familial relationships and events, anchors our sense of place in time. As life reaches toward the light, in equal measure it penetrates deep into the dark soil of our past. Human evolution, our hopes, dreams, and fears, all sustain our common ground. Observe, listen, and learn from the messages that speak through ancestral links. Invite the past to show itself and reveal a path for you to walk with integrity.

Rather than "fixing" your life, begin to explore your history; it will reveal the deeply interwoven patterns that make up your lineage. Over eons, these interwoven roots have grown strong, fed by the joys and sorrows of your ancestors. By relaxing into your ground of being, you will see that every person, plant, animal, and mineral—all of existence, really— is part of you.

We focus on the visible
the short-lived, accountable
while beneath our feet
dusty with earth and history
the grass grows green
nourished by ancient mists
that rise from the depths
with secrets hidden for a million years.
Plunge your arms into that teeming soil
join hands in sweet entanglement
relieve the burden of your isolation
with the company of those who walked your path before
and know you as you are.

·· 2 ··
BE HERE NOW

L IVING A YES TO LIFE means accepting that sorrow and pain are counterparts to joy and pleasure. Evading this reality keeps us hoping that fulfillment is possible while denying the nature of existence. And when that doesn't work, as it cannot in the very nature of things, we foolishly wonder, "Why me?"

Our minds love to ping-pong between memory and fantasy, between scenarios that are alternately yummy, upsetting, fearful, marvelous. Like a dog with a favorite bone, we dig up our past for yet another chew, utterly unaware of the living, breathing, tail-wagging experience of *now*.

By neglecting what each moment offers, we sleep-walk, bump into life, and get shocked when it hurts. Yet,what is imagined, dreamed, and believed is just a fraction of the truth of *what is*—and far less important than turning the attention of the one who is lost in thoughts to the present.

This isn't to say that we should negate what was, deny nostalgia, or forsake all dreams of the future—by all means go there, *but* maintain awareness of your present self when digging into the past for material to project imagined futures.

Being here now accepts the eternal and ever-changing present. A subtle and profound healing awareness lies within the simplicity of living THIS . . . and now THIS!

I am struck by the delightfully fierce pulling of my attention into the present that my Luna the Pooch brings to every moment we are together. And how remarkable a gift to have an animal friend teach about being present during these most difficult times, when the mind easily slips into revisiting the past and/or jumping madly into an imagined future.

·· 3 ··
COOPERATION

THE NATURAL WORLD EXISTS because of interdependence. The whole spectrum of life, from the minuscule to the mighty, is critical to our well-being. Sunlight and stars, soil and water, animals and plants, microbes and moonlight . . . their mixing and mingling are essential for life to thrive.

Old ways of thinking based on competition, going it alone, and thinking only of ourselves have cut us off from nature's life-sustaining intelligence. If musicians in an orchestra compete to be heard above each other or insist on equal performance time, the outcome will be chaos. Each artist's contribution is vital to the symphony.

Now, more than ever, we face a time when cooperation is essential. That doesn't mean we must sacrifice our uniqueness or individuality. Nature is all-inclusive. Diversity nourishes resilience; variety strengthens and enhances the whole.

Cooperation is a mighty force. Grounded, unified voices and efforts can turn mountains into molehills!

Survival on this beautiful planet depends upon respect for nature, the many diverse cultures and their histories, and each other, while sharing our unique gifts that support health and well-being for all. Our future depends on each of us joining hands and hearts and taking next steps together.

One of the greatest needs and pleasures as a human is to share something that is really special and works for you. I rub one drop of bergamot oil on my belly to awaken my soul to hope and courage, bringing self-acceptance and alignment. In the morning, two drops of cedarwood on my feet manifest the right people in my life. These two essential earth oils diffused with frankincense invite new perspectives based on light and truth.

·· 4 ··
CONSUMING

UNCHECKED CONSUMERISM, the unrestrained need for gratification, is killing us. And in our self-serving pursuit to have ever more stuff, we are killing the planet as well.

It's not that we haven't alerted ourselves to the pitfalls of what we're doing. "Bigger isn't always better," we say. "Money can't buy you love." But these folk wisdoms have become clichés without real meaning.

Our world's consumer societies thrive on human appetites,

desires, and insecurities about ourselves and life in general. We've come to believe that if we just take this pill, upgrade our device, or own a certain car, our persistent discomfort—that nagging feeling of emptiness—will vanish. Our childish expectations demand that the Earth serve our whims, soothe our angst, and keep us entertained.

Would you unplug yourself from consuming if you knew, firsthand, that it is setting your home ablaze? Would you hoard if you saw that it injured the life of your child, your pet . . . or decimated oceans and forests? Does the idea of less-is-more feel like a trick, irritate you, make you angry? If so, ask yourself, *WHY?*

Self-indulgence is generally incapable of discerning when enough is enough. Its recklessness gets jolted to reality only when faced with near insurmountable problems.

If increase feels burdensome rather than beneficial, it signals a time to change tack and bring the issue of sustainability home, where it belongs. By making some tough choices today, we sow seeds in support of generations to come. Be inspired, get creative, think outside of the box!

I firmly believe that we all need to find something to do in our lives that stops us from eating the couch.

·· 5 ··
PERSEVERANCE

THIS SMALL BIRD MUST GATHER all her resources to meet the difficult challenges she is facing.

The world feels harsh and hostile when things fail to go as planned. Staying alive in what seems to be a frozen landscape, where everything is hibernating, cloaked, and unwelcoming, requires backbone, ingenuity, and determination.

Such times are stressful and exhausting, especially when the desire to break free of uncertainty grows stronger and the longing for the comforts of better days creates sadness and worries. In tough times, when facing the stark reality of diminishing resources, be gentle and forgiving to yourself. By simplifying, eliminating the stressors that deplete and create depression, you change crippling old patterns that have fed you feelings of unworthiness and being cast out in the cold. Focus on tending your inner flame. Realign yourself with whatever encourages love and respect. Steer your attention away from external events and you will bring awareness back home to the here and now, where it belongs. Trust that life is taking care, even when it hurts.

Working with limitations takes patience and awareness that life is a process in which hidden strengths are revealed, especially during times of austerity. Once spring returns, and it will, you'll appreciate this endurance test. In fact, the trials of life are meant to strengthen us to brave hardship with a bounce-back resilience that infuses every part of our being.

When the time is right, the road is wide—until then, keep a low profile, stoke the fire, and put the kettle on.

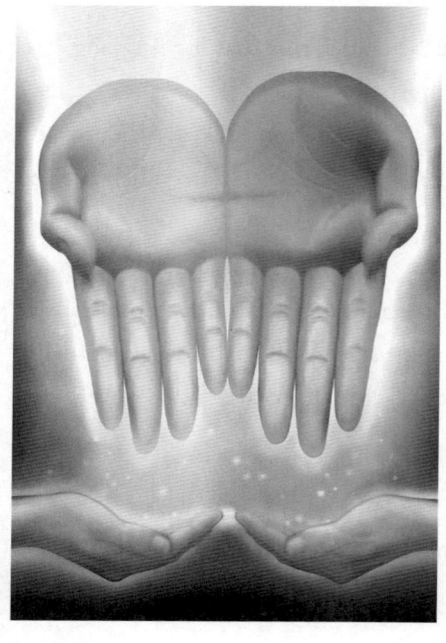

·· 6 ··
GENEROSITY

T HE EVER-TURNING WHEEL OF LIFE spins in a natural exchange of energies: emptiness invites fullness; fullness empties out. In human terms, it's about give and take, offering and receiving, abundance and scarcity. By living in accordance with these cycles, we avoid getting stuck in one-sided thinking that aims to modify the natural flow.

When generosity is advertised, put on display, know well that it is motivated by something other than open-handed sharing. The publicity is meant to conceal a less attractive, hidden agenda. Such "gifts" tend to come with conditions (explicit or implicit) that create indebtedness, with all the humiliation and resentment that can bring.

If you look deeper into the "small print" of any act that is promoted as doing you a favor, you may find an array of unspoken requirements that must be met prior to the generous offer taking place. When transactions appear too good to be true, there is every possibility that the hand extended toward you is actually on the take.

Giving openly, without conditions, is a blessing. Receptivity to what is offered is also a blessing. This interdependent, balanced transfer of energy takes nothing for granted and is truly a win-win experience for all. Life is not about handouts. When something is given, something is taken—you can bank on it!

My childhood did not render me generous, but as an adult I've witnessed the magic of giving.
One New Year's Day, my toll on the Golden Gate Bridge was anonymously paid by the car ahead of me.
The experience left me exhilarated and hopeful. The following year I paid the fair of
the one behind and was surprised to experience an even greater thrill.

·· 7 ··
TIMING

THERE IS LITTLE DIFFERENCE in the maturation process of a plant or a person. For both, there are stages when the safe and familiar must be shed. Becoming never returns to what was.

When our usual coping styles no longer serve us, there is a gap when everything feels disconnected, vulnerable. That unnerving space is a dynamic trigger for change.

Observe the shifting emotional climate within yourself and those around you. Observe how the mind translates difficulties as problems because they slow progress, disrupting our preferences and plans.

When life tests us, it signals imminent change is at hand that cannot be ignored. After the unexpected, growth and innovation are sure to follow. As the old undergoes this makeover, tune in to the bigger picture.

Awkward times are perfect for clarifying objectives, strengthening core values, and birthing new ways of living and being. Respect the wisdom of life; its timing is not a hit-or-miss affair. Be gentle with yourself and others. Every life is a work in progress; there is no free pass for avoiding the gritty stuff, no bouquet for growing up. Inner flowering arises out of trial and error, weathering storms, and overcoming obstacles; it is how strong roots take hold and wisdom arises. This flowering is you.

All life is in synchronicity with Nature. Trusting Her timing opens us, despite the difficulties.
Listening to the rhythm of your heart reveals an incredible beauty and strength.

Violet is the color of wholeness, when the dualities of life—vulnerable and strong, giving and receiving, yin and yang—
are expressed together in this small flower. Relaxed, totally connected to essence, there can be no wrong timing.

·· 8 ··
LABOR OF LOVE

Throughout history, certain individuals have devoted themselves to creativity and to manifesting the inexpressible. Yet raw talent isn't enough to skillfully give form and substance to inspiration; it must be practiced, refined, become second nature. Developing one's talent requires passion, hits and misses, and plenty of repetition.

In a dimension outside of time, full of heart and mystery, the creator works toward manifesting their gifts. For some, it is in response to a deep inner calling; for others, it is a devotional, an offering. For a few, it is a gripping force that wrings out their blood, sweat, and tears onto the page, canvas, stage. What is common to all is the essential need to make art.

Mastering our art requires dedicating significant amounts of solitary time for working. This necessity, whether your own or someone's you know, should be respected without pressure, coercion, demands for tidying up, or expectations to produce.

Appreciate what you or others accomplish in the multidimensional, infinitely faceted realm of artistic expression. By honing your craft, focusing on the work at hand, this time is yours—not for what others think. Producing for the marketplace isn't the message here; rather, it is to respect the commitment it takes to realize one's art and, in so doing, fulfill a sacred calling.

I always feel that creativity is an open channel to the unknown. It requires surrounding yourself with inspiration and letting something flow out of it. Ultimately, you gain mastery from having learned how to navigate the mistakes and blockages on your path. Then the freedom to create is upon you! Ah, the joy and wonder of such a moment brings blessings to you and the world.

ᵥᵥ 9 ᵥᵥ
SATISFACTION

THIS BIG CAT HAS LEARNED BY TRIAL AND ERROR how to excel in her field. In every endeavor, she aims for being the best, yet she is the first to admit that refusal of second best can mean missing out altogether.

Her respected position attracts both envy and criticism that she accepts as part of the territory. She enjoys flexing her skills and with a Cheshire cat grin admits to loving a good challenge that keeps her at the top of her game.

For this individual, home is a sanctuary that emphasizes

her natural elegance and singular lifestyle. If partnered, she maintains her autonomy. Her satisfaction comes from having mastered the chops to achieve the positive outcome she's worked hard for, and with all the boxes ticked, she enjoys the comforts of a life well lived.

She holds those who express ingenuity and fortitude in high regard, even when they encroach on her territory. She is generous and supportive if she senses a need, but she remains unmoved when approached by those seeking to take advantage of her.

As this force of nature dreams of broadening her prospects, she appraises her many accomplishments, while enjoying the fragrance of roses and savoring a well-deserved bowl of cream.

I see the fierce, unrelenting determination in her eyes, coupled naturally with this languid-sensual
pure cat quality that relishes licking the bowl. As women, we are often asked to choose between equal
but opposite aspects of ourselves, between the masculine and feminine, the active and receptive.
But why choose when we are both? Domesticity and ferocity are twin souls within her skin.
That is her truest ground, her highest skill, and her deepest satisfaction.

·· 10 ··
PRIVILEGE

THE CLOSED EYES AND IRON GATES of privilege threaten as much as they defend. Nowadays, hardship, loss, and the grief that follows in its wake are undeniably encroaching into the lives of people everywhere.

This card depicts a status that for eons has been revered but is now way past its expiration date—a superfluous dinosaur. Planet Earth is undergoing a housecleaning, ringing the death knell on every self-aggrandizing, privileged abuse of her land, seas, air, and every great and small creature who calls this Earth home. Privileged thinking has fanned the flames of social, economic, and environmental disasters everywhere. As Mother Nature heals herself, we witness that much of what is lived for today will simply be gone tomorrow, and it hurts like hell. Working in accord to ensure that we have a future, joining hands, hearts, and resources, we equally must accept the responsibility and the privilege of being human.

I am painfully aware how privilege shapes our lives and our stories about ourselves and others. I also know that we are comprised of what we love, what we value, and what we disdain, all tangled up inside of ourselves. Given different life circumstances and opportunities, I might be the one running into that burning building, or the one lighting the fire, the one attempting to put it out, or even the one who may show some kindness to any who safely walked away.

There is a very strong possibility that we will get many chances in the coming times to test our mettle, our swords, and our hearts' capacity to stay open in the face of hardship, suffering, and the challenge of living in "interesting times."

·· 11 ··
HONESTY

THE HONEST EGG we all recognize is essentially perfect, containing both untapped potential and great nourishment. Its innate simplicity needs no embellishment. In human terms, the honest eggs are unpretentious persons of integrity who are simply at home in themselves. Their uncomplicated, clear-cut manner and tell-it-like-it-is approach needs no elaboration.

Typically, the introverted ordinary eggs of our world are overlooked amid the splendid, extroverted ones. But there are times when their quiet approach is what is most needed, and that can have a reassuring influence. This card calls for simplifying, appreciating moderation, and becoming aware of the seemingly insignificant little things. Pay attention to the perspective offered by a no-nonsense person of integrity who will tell it like it is, even if it hurts.

If you are looking to make friends and influence others and what you stand for isn't favored by popular opinion, then forthrightness will likely be a problem—for outspoken honesty is off-putting to those who expect a polished presentation that appeals to the status quo before they will listen.

When the time for small talk is over, truthfulness is what is called for. If it causes your standing to diminish in the eyes of others, so be it. Turn their dismissal into an opportunity to shed any fears you may have of not being good enough, smart enough, sophisticated, educated, or important enough. Instead, focus inward to acknowledge and respect your own truth. Your authenticity is more than sufficient. It is luminous.

Honestly, it's been a very distracting week, and I'm not able to focus well. All I can say is that in my life, honesty delivered gently has paved the way for intimacy and trust.

·· 12 ··
EXPLORE

FEELING BORED, STUCK IN A RUT, is a sign that the fear of insecurity is putting the brakes on living your life. When the longing to broaden your horizon comes up, it should not be ignored. The pull to break free on any number of fronts—social, physical, creative, spiritual—may have been tugging at your heart for some time. We conjure up a host of reasons and distractions to muffle the call of the wild. But when we suppress that urge, we become complacent, indifferent—living fragmented lives that affect our body and its energy, our thinking, and both our daytime and dreamtime experiences.

Exploring is energizing and liberating, a chance to learn more of yourself and the world around you. Whether you seek truth, adventure, or a break from the status quo, you are asking for a fresh approach that will enhance your life. The adventure of exploring is exhilarating and is vastly enriched when undertaken with respectful, observant openness. Then, whatever path you take will eventually lead toward self-realization and wisdom.

I stepped out at a very young age to discover the world. I left home in New York City to go west, to sleep under the stars, to sleep on Mother Earth, to gaze upon high mountains and open spaces, and to see who I am without the burdens of safety, familiarity, and sameness.

I found my way to the UK to study ancient medical arts, leaving the dream of traditional medical study behind. Following a strong voice inside me, I journeyed to India to imbibe ancient wisdom and to explore my deepest self.

·· 13 ··
SUPPORT

THIS EARTH MAMA'S HOME serves as a refuge for friends from every walk, flutter, and swim of life. In defense of loved ones—or her principles—she can be formidable, and she will not back down unless proven wrong. Then, any hard feelings are dissolved by an invitation to dinner, a pipe of peace, or both.

She chafes at small-mindedness and can sniff out deceit however well it is concealed. In support of a worthy cause, no stone is left unturned. She doesn't seek attention or praise for her generosity but will accept it when it serves the greater good.

Some aspects of her nature can be seen in the conscientiousness of bees. Queen or drone, each plays a vital role in maintaining the hive. Without even trying, their energy provides for not only the plant kingdom but much of the natural world.

This card portrays one who attentively monitors changes in the environment and strives to maintain the health and well-being of the planet. By focusing on quality over quantity, she supports the entire Earth family—she regards this as a responsibility toward future generations.

Surrounded by the abundance of Mother Earth, a nurturing woman embraces an endangered koala,
who nestles into her like a grandchild. Through this simple act, she is mothering all of Existence.
Relaxed within her arms, the koala is every child, nurtured and safe, in a tender embrace.
The reciprocal exchange of trust and love heals and supports both, bringing wholeness and peace.
It is the simple beauty of interdependence in all of life.

·· 14 ··
RESPECT

His Green Man, as he shelters an endangered baby bird, expresses a guardianship of compassionate concern. His watchful presence conveys a no-nonsense approach to changing conditions in the natural world that is born from down-to-earth experience and hard work. His manner communicates the urgent need to address and correct the abuse of Earth's seas, lands, and atmosphere.

This gentle soul is a pragmatist who knows that without preparing the ground and maintaining a sincere commitment, no amount of hope or good intentions will make the changes needed to ensure a healthy future for all of Earth's children. He does not broadcast his message, yet many have rallied to his cause and work passionately in support of it.

Respect for life is the theme here, beseeching you to spend time in nature, plant a garden, gather medicinal herbs, or relax on a hillside and with a long, slow breath feel the vibrant healing pulse of everything around you. Involvement in conservation, environmental work, or animal welfare is supported.

Be guided by these capable hands with living dirt beneath their nails, while they expertly reveal how and where to plant seeds that nourish and create positive change.

Mother Earth has plenty of light, heat, and sun's rays. She also needs deep soil, wetlands, more forests, and moist, dark places. By equating darkness with evil, unconsciousness, and light with open-hearted awareness, we misunderstand nature. Darkness is where life begins; nothing exists without it. Our body's surface is small compared to the vast, wet darkness within us. Recognize equally the unconsciousness and consciousness of humankind with compassionate awareness. As old constructs disintegrate, let them compost the garden of Mother Earth.

FIRE

*Suit of energy, ambition, courage, inspiration,
creativity, willpower, and intensity,
commonly known as the suit of wands.*

·· 1 ··
INSPIRATION

MOMENTS OF INSPIRATION ARE EXCEPTIONAL. They flash unexpectedly, like a comet streaking across the night sky, and they initiate change. The bright ideas spawned by inspiration accelerate growth, expand vision, and bring clarity.

This brilliant occasion is ripe with potential that supercharges thinking outside the box, setting the stage for something utterly unique to take shape. Stimulating new concepts will break through old patterns while clarifying something previously left in the dark, vague, or in doubt. What once seemed impossible can now be faced with renewed energy and a greater sense of purpose. You are empowered to tread confidently into uncharted territory, and in doing so, you will inspire others to follow your lead. Aha moments like this are life-changing events that set wheels and brainwaves in motion. Such occurrences have been described as a stroke of genius, a bolt from the blue, an epiphany.

Though the source of inspiration remains shrouded, its stimulating potential is quickening something to manifest through you.

Enlightened thought effortlessly shines without prejudice or preference. For millennia, inspired individuals who have shared the light of their understanding have changed the course of history. Your inspired perception can offer a fresh approach, creating a brighter day for yourself and many others.

Inspiration is the act of breathing the divine into the body. Part of my practice involves working with dancers as both a teacher and choreographer and acting as a catalyst for them to remember their beauty. Through opening into inspired experience, the body expresses its sacred nature in a myriad of ways. This is fierce grace that demands the fire of courage to fully surrender to inspiration that arises from the unknowable depths of being.

·· 2 ··
FOCUS

T HIS OWL'S OBJECTIVE IS FULLY FOCUSED on finding a rich hunting ground to use her considerable skills. Her sights are set on attaining excellence by exposing weakness, improving conditions and uncovering facts.

Owls represent wisdom and keen observation that prevent them from becoming emotionally tangled up in small-minded pursuits. They conserve energy and wait for the moment they sense is right to make a move—when all their efforts will pay off. Sharp-eyed awareness empowers her to avoid traps that ensnare less practiced others. As an ally, she is designed for the job of oversight, identifying what has previously been hidden or camouflaged to befuddle or distract.

Hold the vision of achieving your goal and strategize how to attain it. As you proceed, trust your instincts, tend to detail, and ignore alluring prospects that pop up along the way. Seek out better hunting grounds to feel empowered and inspired. Your uncanny ability to spot little things, that upon closer scrutiny are found to be important, stirs up envy or mistrust in others. Don't let their side-glances steer you away from your focus. You've come too far to get caught up in pettiness. Aim high. And note that with increased confidence comes greater responsibility.

Clear up unfinished business before you move on. By freeing yourself from an entangled hindrance, you'll know how to avoid similar traps in the future. Once freed from preoccupation with the past, you'll move swiftly toward all that you so richly deserve.

Open wide the scope of your viewing glass, knowing that love is the path, the pathfinder,
and the ultimate fulfillment. Focus on this and never waver.

··· 3 ···

REFRESH

RENEWAL IS A NATURAL PROCESS that happens around and within us with every breath we take. However, over time we develop an outer shell, a mask of affectation meant to protect us from the trials of life. Identification with that mask can harden us—at the expense of staying in touch with our innately trusting nature.

In fact, fresh beginnings are available throughout all the days of our lives. That untarnished presence, our inner child, always remains available—but the refreshing outlook of innocence is often neglected or ignored and considered inappropriate or naive. We refresh our devices, but rarely do we refresh our thinking, preferring to stick with what is already known.

Restoring contact with one's inner child begins by dropping the constant need to be "on top of it" and knowledgeable about absolutely everything—including what lies ahead! A restorative process is unleashed when we trust. We become responsive rather than reactive. It is a shift in awareness that is nothing less than a rebirth into wonder, and it is possible at any age. It can be a little scary. Once a seed's shell breaks open, there is no turning back. And we grow as we imbibe the rich mulch of all our days and nights, trials and errors, successes and failures. Nobody is ever a finished product.

This is a powerful reminder of our immortality, and, more importantly, acknowledges the virtue that remains a child within all of us. Whatever we perceive or experience is first seen through the eyes of our inner child that connects, heals, and responds with the purity and goodness of innocence.

·· 4 ··
DANCE

DANCE IS INTEGRAL TO LIFE. Our bodies remember the rhythmic heartbeat that initiated our first buoyant response within the womb.

Sometimes, amid the routines of life, an impulse stirs us, summoned by a melody in the marketplace, the patter of rainfall, and the dancer inside responds—tapping her feet, stimulated, animated, and alive. The motivation to dance harkens back to a time before time when our ancestors communicated, venerated life, and shared stories through rhythmic movement. When that primordial instinct is activated, the body, mind, heart, and soul all unite. It is dance that connects us to our roots, each other, the past, present, and future.

By moving the body rhythmically with feet fully in touch with the ground or spontaneously extending an arm to sweep through space, movement reactivates the genius of our body's innate language. There is no right or wrong way to dance your vibrant inner light, your unfathomable depths, and all the emotional spaces in between.

The freedom of dance restores vitality. Like clouds parting, it reveals a freshness that was missing just moments before. Rediscovering your inner dancer becomes a reunion with a beloved from long ago, bringing tears or laughter or a profound stillness—knowing you've come home to yourself.

If you have lost sight of your light, it can feel risky coaxing it from the place where it hides.
Patience, even devotion, is called for to find and then restore what was lost. Begin again.
One moment at a time, one step at a time. We can dance just as we live. Focusing on well-being
may seem like a luxury, but it is one we cannot afford to ignore. Find your dance!

·· 5 ··
COMPETITION

No child is born a competitor. The drive to outperform and defeat others is taught. Yes, every child enjoys mastering new skills, learning a new game, being "best in class" in spelling or math. But when winning is the only way to get love or approval, and losing brings shame and criticism, the joy of self-mastery is crippled.

When children are taught that winning is all that matters, a path toward becoming a ruthless adult may ensue. For some, the need for love warps into a drive to come out on top, regardless of the pain it causes. In others, performance anxiety affects every aspect of their lives, as the fear of being a loser prevents them from taking risks, exploring new terrain, reaching out to a friend.

The kill-or-be-killed games of ancient Rome are gone, but those ferocious competitions are still active in our collective unconscious and play out in today's world—to the point that we celebrate the winners and honor them as heroes, even when they do appalling things. Redirect your attention away from dwelling on the achievements of others toward realigning with your inner child, who simply enjoys innocent play. This releases any pressure you feel to live up to bigger-than-life expectations. Self-respect honors your innate abilities above your achievements. You are stellar, no matter what.

We are birthing a new humanity. By moving into finer levels of awareness and sensitivity, demeaning competition has no place. The Awakened Feminine is a paradigm recognizing that our purpose is to uplift each other and all humanity.

Life is abundant; there is more than enough to go round. Earth could become a paragon of love, support, contribution, and collaboration.

·· 6 ··
TRIUMPH

ATTAINING A HIGH POINT in any endeavor of life is the result of steady improvement, focus, perseverance, and many factors that are beyond your control. A striking result doesn't happen overnight. And despite the temptation to push the process, there are no guarantees that a juicy conclusion will be reached at all.

Excellence arises from making intelligent choices within an ever-widening field of alternatives. Often, combining diverse sources that encourage teamwork and inspiration brings the most rewarding outcomes. Such opportunities can show up out of the blue from unexpected places way outside your comfort zone.

Whenever the "sweet smell of success" wafts your way, the atmosphere can become charged with elation, relief, and an appetite for more of all the good stuff. Be aware that these feelings can be intoxicating—to the point you can easily lose touch with the deeply felt sense of meaning and purpose you had when you began. This success might have remained just a dream were it not for the support of others who believed in you and encouraged you along the way.

When I was writing novels, it was deeply satisfying to come to the end of a sentence and realize that, yes, the book was finished. I worked on one book for eight years before chucking out everything and starting again. Having it accepted by a publisher was the beginning of all the stress that comes from the "sweet smell of success"—comparison, wildly optimistic fantasies about praise, fame, and glory! Working with small documentary films in the past decades and sharing the wisdom and beauty of the people I film is deeply satisfying. Much more so than the ungrounded fantasies of youth.

·· 7 ··
ADAPTABILITY

ADAPTABLE, SHAPESHIFTING, SELF-POSSESSED, the fox holds the fire of life within her swiftly moving form. Whatever the weather, this creature meets it with gusto in her every leap, dash, and fully alert pause.

An opportunistic charmer, the fox takes what she wants and magically disappears, unencumbered by others who would love to keep her company for just a little longer. She reserves her affections for her nearest kin and a collection of trusted friends who have shown fortitude and resilience through hard times. When days of plenty arise in spring, her changing coat becomes vivid, merging into the multicolored landscape, protecting her advantage while furthering nature's wild purpose. Now you see her, now you don't, and any glimpse confers a flash of otherworldly grace.

This card is an invitation to tend the fire that burns within you. Existence put it there to spur your canny, self-regarding instinct to keep going, seize the moment, survive, and thrive. Confidence, alertness, and instinctive timing fuel the staying power needed to complete an undertaking while still maintaining a healthy reserve of energy. The fox's undaunted nature is helpful when you find yourself on a rough patch of ground. Undisturbed by life's challenges, her adaptability succeeds where others fail. Independent and confident, she instinctively knows when charm or a lowered profile is all that is needed to win the day.

A mime mirrors life and the characters that pass through it. As a performance artist, I am a kind of shapeshifter who keenly observes and assumes the persona of others, reflecting them back to themselves. Improvisation has taught me to adapt, in the moment, while "thinking on my feet." Adaptability is my art form.

·· 8 ··
SELF-CONFIDENCE

THIS WOMAN HAS JUMPED through hoops of fire, meeting and mastering many challenges. Now her skills are honed, and she is in full, dynamic movement—confident and unafraid. More hurdles are sure to come, but her resolve is strong enough to meet them straight on. Whatever goal has been set in motion is finally within reach, and to attain it, her focused energy will utilize everything she's got.

With the dynamic intensity of this card, you must stay

alert—be ready to leap at a moment's notice—because more change is imminent! You've come a long way. As you reflect on the challenges you've passed through, acknowledge all those who have encouraged your progress. Their confidence has fostered your own.

Don't turn delays into obstacles. The holy grail of what you've been seeking is in sight! Everything furthers. You're in tip-top form, focused, and fully motivated. Acknowledge your inner strength. The "Force" is with you.

When I left home to attend university, a quest to gain confidence in myself began. Only later, at sixty-nine, did I face my first trial by fire in the form of breast cancer surgery. It unleashed much insecurity. I realized that my self-confidence was adopted from my parents, but I knew nothing of my own personal confidence. When facing life's challenges, and doubts arise, I recognize that old lack of confidence in myself. Then I dive deeper and reclaim what is always within reach. I am so very grateful for every experience that has supported me to remember that I am worthy and can stand up and make a difference not only in my own life but in the lives of others.

RESISTANCE

MAINTAINING A WALL OF RESISTANCE is a demanding, full-time job. The endless need to shore up one's defenses is not only exhausting, it creates an atmosphere of unnecessary tension and continual discontent. Eventually, the inflexibility portrayed here will either shift or entirely break down from the persistent nature of change that is life.

Resistance tactics like gaslighting or diverting attention elsewhere are other methods to manipulate, distract, or overwhelm the opposition. Creating discord to bolster one's position, or threaten the "enemy," is a strategy used by bullies to impose their will on others and divert resources for their own gain.

Once a position becomes hardened, the flow of communication is blocked. Depending upon the extent of a stalemate, it may be necessary to reframe the dialogue entirely. Cooler heads, with an unbiased viewpoint, can help restore a calmer and more respectful atmosphere.

A balanced exchange needs trust, flexibility, and a healthy respect for differing points of view. When opposing forces are open and transparent, cheating or manipulating is difficult. If you are called on to navigate such a tough situation, remember that it takes a steady, confident, nonthreatening approach. Think of water eroding rock—its strength is in its constancy that gradually wears down hardness without losing its own integrity. Alternatively, by expressing its natural tendency to seek low ground, flowing water continues its watercourse way to finally arrive at journey's end.

When after a lifetime of carving I finally put down my hammer and chisel, I saw that in truth, it was the stones that split me open. They gradually shaped me by wearing away my hard edges and by softening my approach to life.

·· 10 ··
OVERLOAD

FEELING BURDENED, FRUSTRATED, AND PRESSURED can be toxic. Once it becomes habitual, it's a recipe for collapse. Taking on more than you can handle often begins innocently, by lending a hand or doing a favor. However, when helpfulness is motivated by a need for recognition or approval, it becomes a trap that weakens the ability to deliver on important commitments, especially those that strengthen your self-respect.

Stress management begins with sussing out the root cause

of what on the surface appears to be selfless behavior but leaves you feeling drained, unappreciated, and abused. It signals a deeper compulsion that needs to be seen for what it is.

Look into your beliefs concerning indebtedness or responsibility and what makes a good son, daughter, parent, spouse, employee, or friend. If being obedient or always saying yes is how you express loyalty or love, drop it. The inability to say no is soul-crushing. It festers into unrelenting disappointment with life, and ultimately with oneself. Honesty includes the ability to simply say no at times, while it establishes personal boundaries. Once you can refuse, decline, reject with self-respect, your yes will have real meaning. Otherwise, it's just a symptom of emotional servitude. Actualizing your self-respect makes all the difference.

The spotlight here is on the need to change unconscious patterns regarding an unchecked desire to serve or be helpful. Initially, this inner work can feel like opening a tightly closed fist. At first it aches and seems impossible, but with persistence, the tension relaxes, and flexibility is restored.

You don't have to earn it. You don't have to prove it.
You don't have to bargain for it. You don't have
to beg for it. You are worthy. Worthy.
Simply because you exist.

·· 11 ··
SELF-EXPRESSION

OR MILLENNIA, HUMANS HAVE EVOLVED language, symbolism, and art. We express ourselves by giving form, voice, and rhythm to our dreams, hopes, and fears. Yet today, for many of us, self-expression is rarely undertaken with purpose.

As a rule, modern culture discourages creative pursuits, deeming them an unnecessary waste of time, space, and money. In much of the world, creatives must choose between staying within the lines of acceptability or abandoning the security of the status quo. For too many, unexplored self-expression becomes a hidden source of regret.

Rekindling the creative fire can initially feel daunting, and if it does, remember that entering the realm of self-expression—by facing an empty canvas, dance floor, or keyboard—is sure to get the heart racing.

Whether that fluttering heart arises out of fear or excitement, don't let it stop you. If creative pursuits seem mad or selfish, remember that this very personal process sparks enthusiasm for life and empowers self-respect.

Summon your muse now. She awaits acceptance of her invitation to play. This card urges you to creatively, and with gusto, express something of yourself. Age, appropriateness, and a polished skill set are irrelevant here. Give yourself full permission to mess about and discover.

When I'm uninspired, I renew the creative flow by drawing something I love . . . Eventually channels unblock by themselves; inspiration descends. I challenge myself with new techniques to keep it all alive. When I'm out of control and don't know what I'm doing, that vast, wild flow really pours— the work creates itself. I just start and don't fret over the outcome. Just start. Inspiration will find you.

·· 12 ··
INTENTION

BY FOCUSING ALL SENSES FULLY, VIVIDLY, to a point where every aspect of your objective is distinct—you can smell, taste, and touch it—nothing can steer you off course. When love is the motivator, a wholehearted vision radiates straight from the core of being, bright like the sun, from which warmth and courage emanate.

Optimism is empowering a burst of energy that steps up the pace in every area of life. There is no looking back. Your true purpose is luminous, clear, and bright, lighting the way to manifest a cherished vision.

It is love that defines how we relate to the world, how we are perceived by others, and ultimately how we reach our highest calling. When talents and abilities are strengthened by personal integrity and inspired by the heart and its aim, sooner or later, the goal is reached. This card illustrates a perfectly aligned intense effort achieving success. That excellent moment may come with a drum roll or a silent inner smile. However, when we recognize that our personal energies contributed to positive change, the effect is enduring.

It is a blessing to be guided by this fierce spirit. Her wildness has nurtured, protected, and kept me strongly alive. Over many decades, my medicine and health-giving practice has been aligned to this dynamic life force that is expressed from my heart, directing the arrows of love, compassion, and healing toward scores of people around the world. To continue learning, exploring, bringing knowledge and well-being to those who can receive it is the goal of these virtues.

This is discriminating intention; listen, express your truth, do not waste words and wisdom on closed minds and ears.

·· 13 ··
SPONTANEITY

THIS VIBRANT PERSONALITY has a staunch, don't-mess-with-me core. She is self-confident, curious about life, an expert multitasker without skipping a beat. She's a mom, businesswoman, fundraiser, and activist and expresses herself creatively in a variety of pursuits to the benefit of her family, friends, and community.

When challenged, she can be a fierce opponent who stands her ground. There's no half-heartedness in this one; she gives her all and expects others to do the same. Her personal magnetism can even sway those who once opposed her.

This high-frequency energy refuses to be stifled. When faced with a lukewarm reception, she moves on. Her falcon mask symbolizes an innate ability to home in on anything she sets her sights on. With an uncanny knack for engaging an audience, she exudes considerable power. An intense competitor, she has high expectations of herself and anyone taken under her wing. Such an inspiring individual can be intimidating; occasionally her forthrightness is misinterpreted as arrogance. When backlash occurs, she can leave others in the dust feeling abandoned, taken for granted, or ignored.

For all the success this card brings, it comes with a few reminders: be aware of the impact you have on others, respect alternative viewpoints, and get plenty of rest to avoid burning out.

I sometimes throw thunderbolts in a moment of passion, or I can be the most supportive of allies. Starting projects or launching new ideas is second nature. In the fullness of time, the ability to bring them to completion has come to me as well. Don't be afraid to start! You may find amazing treasures on the road, and failure is only another bend in your path to true self-love.

·· 14 ··
INTEGRITY

PERSONS OF INTEGRITY SHINE with a strength of character that emanates confidence and honesty and naturally motivates and inspires others—not out of a need to impress or prove that "might is right," but by their relaxed, respectful, and steady presence.

It is not always easy to stand up for the truth as you see it. But greater awareness of your bottom line strengthens the ability to discern and appreciate sincerity in others, whether you agree with them or not. And you will be surprised to see how often that recognition creates an opening for them to respond in kind.

Be courageous, authentic, without troubling over what others think. No matter what you stand for, there will always be those who condemn or exclude you. So be it. This is your life! Don't waste it on relationships that demand or drain your energy. Seek out those who are in sync with the rhythm of *your* heartbeat.

Look for and weed out any self-defeating concerns that have kept you on the sidelines. Accepting, rather than condemning, your limitations will boost self-confidence while honoring who you are, instead of who you think you should be.

Genuine integrity emits an aura that cannot be feigned and that radiates with a dignity unique to each individual. When vulnerability is accepted as fundamental to growth, compassion for yourself and others strengthens. You come to know that you are vital, not because you have all the answers, but because you have a healthy relationship with what is essential. Then life becomes rich with opportunities—to learn from others, to share your ideas and talents, and to contribute toward supporting the greater good.

If I choose not to speak out of fear, then there's
no one that my silence is standing for.

AIR

*Suit of the intellect, logic, consideration,
refinement, reasoning, beliefs and opinions, and conduct,
commonly known as the suit of swords.*

··1··
CLARITY

A DIAMOND FORMS UNDER PRESSURE, deep within the earth. Dark and lumpy when mined, the stone's unrealized potential can be brought forth only by those who know how to look into its heart. Guided by this perception, each facet is revealed through conscious, meticulous cutting and polishing.

During a lifetime we encounter pressures, many of which seem inescapable, that build into a longing for definition and clarity. Hardships, confusion, disappointments—these are the forces that forge our inner strength and enable clear understanding.

Clear-sightedness does not arise overnight; it comes from an emerging awareness, based in experience, that reveals the mind's tendency to complicate, overthink, and project its own ideas and desires onto reality.

Mindfulness practice helps to establish moment-to-moment awareness while meditation calms the overactive mind. Together, they open us to a view of the clear sky that lies beyond the clouds of our thoughts. In that sky we find a relaxed inner spaciousness that trusts in life rather than troubles over it. A calm centeredness arises when each facet of progress is acknowledged as having been essential for creating wholeness. This time-honored practice is called polishing the diamond.

Every gem is unique; what they all have in common is starting out rough and withstanding multiple pressures and endurance tests until their inner beauty is finally brought to light. The clarity offered now results from polishing your awareness into a treasure that can never be lost.

So fragile and so strong are we. Oh, the beauty and the darkness of this human realm. We are graced and touched by the demands to awaken . . . surrendering with a deep bow to the Mystery over and over again.

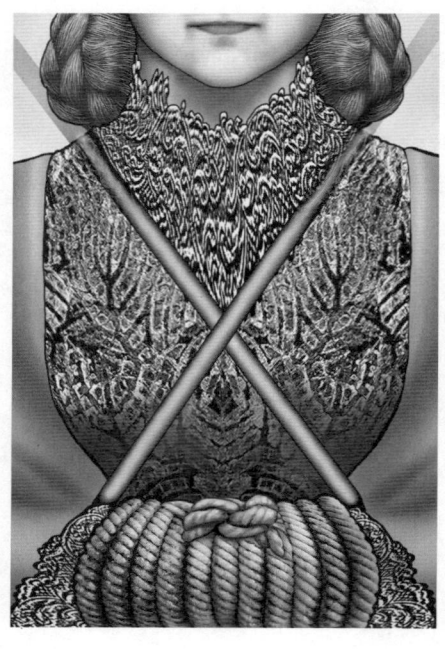

RESTRAINT

O N ONE HAND, restraint limits movement or action. On the other, it can bring relief as it sets up boundaries in order to redirect the flow of our energies into a more integrated and grounded path forward.

Whether a "restraining order" is self-imposed or imposed by an outside source depends entirely on circumstances. But our response to those circumstances, regardless of how they arise, is key.

When the creation of restrictions and boundaries is the

task at hand for you to take on—"I need to restrain myself"—it demands your deepest intelligence and self-knowing. This is an opportunity to understand your own power, see the objective really clearly, and take heed of your gut feelings before proceeding. Unless you can achieve this inner clarity, it might be best to simply withdraw from the situation entirely. If you feel defeated, so be it, but allow the possibility that every process has its timing, and this isn't your time to engage. *The Sacred She* highlights the necessity to know your bottom line.

If the restraints are being imposed on you from the outside, then the same qualities of understanding and owning your inner truth and strength are required. You can't free yourself from unwelcome restrictions by flailing your arms and fighting against them. Do that, and you will only get more entangled in what binds you. Instead, calmly and objectively identify the weak points in the ropes and the chains or the ideas that are holding you down. Then, draw on your inner strength and persistence to develop an unwavering focus on releasing yourself from what constrains you. Sometimes the only way is to painstakingly unravel the knot.

Frustration is not an interruption of your process; frustration is the process.

·· 3 ··
HEARTBREAK

HEARTBREAK AND PAIN dwell in the dark range of our emotional spectrum. We prefer the hues of joy, pleasure, and success, but those colorful peaks cannot exist without the melancholic valleys. These contrasts are fundamental to life—if prosperity, then loss; if birth, death. However dark the valleys, they are essential for developing empathy and wisdom.

When all we hold dear is taken from us, we are cracked open. Over the course of a lifetime, the pain of heartbreak eventually fades, but it never fully disappears. These wounds for some are foundations of courage; for others, suffering and complaint become a way of life.

There is no right way to deal with a broken heart. Accepting the pain it brings can open the door to transformation, while denying it only buries it deeper in the psyche. By accepting and allowing our grief, a profound understanding can arise that is life changing.

Wabi-sabi is a Japanese term that expresses the acceptance of impermanence and imperfection of life and all things. A broken vessel, once mended, is revered for its unique and authentic beauty. Through fully living both our dark and light experiences, we mature.

Let yourself be in this difficult time without suppressing or condemning it. Once the imperceptible beauty of vulnerability is recognized, the heart creates empathy, the vital part that makes us human and therefore divine.

A sensitive heart can break wide open in awe as well as in pain. As it breaks, so can dreams and illusions.
In that freefall back to reality, purification happens from shedding layers of belief, of holding on.
And in letting go a new transparency is revealed—the gift of real seeing.

·· 4 ··
REST

THIS IS A CALL TO RECHARGE your batteries! Existence is telling you to take a break and stop feeling compelled to fill every waking moment. A timely withdrawal is long overdue and essential for restoring balance. Think of it as a backup for your well-being.

Pushing the pause button on work pressures and your daily routine is just as important as keeping appointments and maintaining a schedule. Rarely, if ever, do we prioritize the need for recouping the joy of being alive.

Relaxation is an act of kindness you can give yourself—and you don't have to go anywhere to experience it. Make a sincere commitment to put your feet up by telling others that you are taking it easy—no phone calls, emails, or visits until further notice. Unplug yourself.

Create a space to sit quietly and comfortably, close your eyes, feel the rhythm of your breath moving in, moving out. Look within, review the routines that drive you, and let them go like clouds drifting across the sky.

This meditation offers the experience of your inner world—a calming place to return to whenever you feel the need or are drawn to do so.

Stop running around. Stop Doing. Simply Be. When you know who you are, you relax deeply in the core of your Being, where nothing can rock your boat. Let the waves of sorrow and joy wash over you. They cannot disturb the infinite peace that is your true nature. You are not a transient wave but the ocean— vast, deep, and eternal. Waves come and go, but the essential ocean remains.

·· 5 ··
ARROGANCE

ARROGANCE IS MOST OFTEN A DEFENSIVE PLOY to avoid being seen as weak, ordinary, insignificant. The bluster and posing is an effort to direct attention away from a deep-seated wound of unworthiness and unlovability. The egoist's drive for dominance manifests as an impatient disregard for those they see as beneath them. Always on the defensive, they are constantly on the lookout for "enemies" they fear could threaten their power or diminish their stature. Maintaining such an image demands a staunch belief in their superiority—but propping up that false façade inevitably brings loneliness and alienation. Self-important arrogance creates discord and will never bring harmony and peace.

When confronting arrogant and narcissistic behavior in others, look deeper than the surface. Seek out the shy vulnerability buried within. In the classic children's tale "The Emperor's New Clothes," the king's arrogance only serves his self-deceit. It culminates with an innocent child pointing out the king's nakedness for all to see. The pure simplicity of our inner nature is the common ground of our shared humanity, where nobody is superior or inferior.

Arrogance should not be confused with a truthful straightforwardness that is never aggressive or malicious. Authenticity doesn't need to impress. It is the relaxed quality of being at home in one's own skin, the natural outcome of self-respect and kindness toward oneself and others. It is in understanding that we are connected, in part *because* of our vulnerabilities and our need to touch and be touched, our need to belong, and we share these necessities with much of the natural world.

Arrogance and rudeness are training wheels on the bicycle of life for weak people who cannot keep their balance without them.

·· 6 ··
DEPARTURE

DEPARTING FROM WHAT IS FAMILIAR can be upsetting, even scary. Whether you are leaving your home, job, relationship, or something you have always believed in, when the change is imminent the mind tends to toss up every imaginable possibility: "Maybe things aren't as bad as they seem," or, "Maybe this is a mistake and things will improve, and it's foolish to hope for something better." These seesawing thoughts can stir up just enough confusion to allow you to postpone the inevitable.

The small bird in this card recognizes the need for a timely departure. She understands that her circumstances have changed. She is ready to do whatever is required without second-guessing or looking back. Bluebirds traditionally represent happiness, and the leaf she carries from her past into her future symbolizes her journey toward a fresh start. That leafy reminder will be woven into her new nest and serve as a memento of where she comes from.

Transition periods are always fraught with uncertainty. But once the process of moving on has gained momentum, it cannot be stopped. Finally, after arriving on new ground, it becomes clear that however uncomfortable it was, making a change was essential. A brighter outlook arises, leaving the stresses of the past far behind.

Trust in the process, spread your wings, and fly toward a new beginning.

Life brings change like the wind. When we accept this truth, it feels surprisingly easy to embrace the natural flow of life toward the unknown—grateful for what has been, listening to the heart, responding to each moment in the here and now is your only guide. Let the winds of change carry you.

·· 7 ··
DECEPTION

ECEIT COMES IN MANY DIFFERENT GUISES. An honest appraisal of your ambitions and manipulative tactics you use to get what you want may bring a revelation. What prompts *your* pretense?

Perhaps you've been deceiving yourself out of a perceived need to appear other than who you are. Maintaining that sham only gets more complicated over time, as the potential glitches in a contrived storyline lurk in the shadows, creating fear of exposure and the condemnation that would follow. You put yourself in a trap, where the only way out is either to further embellish the deception or come clean.

Sometimes deception arises by chance, when an opportune twist of fate makes it possible to profit from another's doubts or difficulties, when previously that seemed impossible. But deception, used to take advantage of others for one's own gain—whether financially, ethically, physically, or spiritually—is a confidence trick, and the results can be devastating.

However successful someone is at pulling the wool over another's eyes, nothing is worth the price of lying to oneself. Dropping duplicitous behavior can alter a legacy of dishonesty.

There is aliveness in this predator's obscured face with pink tongue, glistening teeth, and fiery eyes looking to devour. The lascivious glare is seductive . . . yet it is a face we mistrust. The sheep, by comparison, is blank and dead-eyed, only a cloak to camouflage.

Perhaps maturity provides the wisdom to understand that a sheep's mask is inadequate for hiding a wolf, who seduces out of a need to feed his appetite. A split self that deceives even when he bares his soul. Impossible to love because he is impossible to know; he lies even to himself.

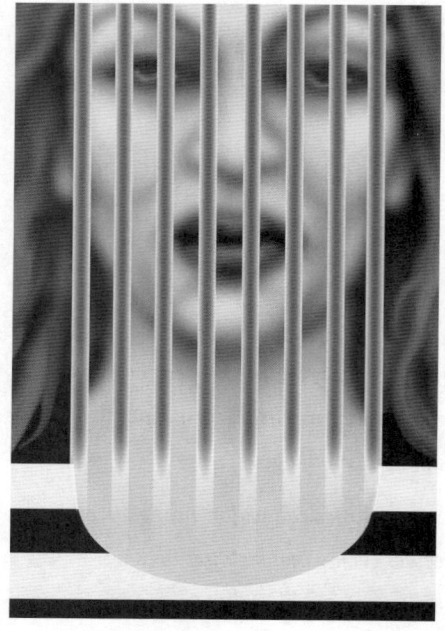

·· 8 ··
BLAME

BLAMING OTHERS OR SCAPEGOATING is how the ego tries to escape accountability—sometimes by playing the victim, other times by gaslighting or claiming the mantle of righteous authority. Self-blame can be a crippling form of guilt, where the condemned and the judge are one and the same.

Before blaming someone or condemning yourself, examine the roots of your opinions and prejudices. These unconscious attitudes have their roots in childhood, when the personality was forming. When a child is caught red-handed reaching into the cookie jar, making up a story to avoid punishment seems an easy way out. Adults often do the same thing when they are caught doing much more serious things. Everyone dreads the embarrassment, shame, or consequences of being caught in the wrong place at wrong time. But once denial and blame become habitual, we never outgrow our childhood expectation and fear of punishment.

Quite simply, this card is about being accountable, taking charge of your actions and reactions. Stop any tendency to blame others for your unhappiness, both in the present and from your past. Take responsibility—that is nobody's job but your own.

One day I finally stopped blaming someone else for my problems. I stopped blaming father, mother, destiny, society, God—for my resistance, my judgments, my self-betrayal. I felt exhausted, drained, spent, and, for the first time, liberated! Free to turn my focus inward and take responsibility for who I am and the life I live, for all the darkness and the light. Also, I stopped blaming myself, and with that, all kinds of inner divisions began dissolving, and a great sense of integration, creativity, and power took its place.

·· 9 ··
FEAR

EAR OF DEATH is a natural and instinctive response to the threat of annihilation that all living creatures share. Humans, however, seem to have a unique capacity to elaborate this primal fear into an extraordinary array of individual dreads and anxieties—fear of failure, rejection, of being helpless, misunderstood, and more. A child's monster under the bed becomes an adult's nightmare of a secret being exposed; a child's encounter with a bully becomes an adult's compulsive need to control. But, as in ordinary nightmares, the storyline is real only if we remain asleep.

Deep-rooted chronic fear is a hangover, a ghost. Whether nurtured by family history, religious upbringing, or the dictates of powerful others, it has been served to us in the past, concocted by those who insist it is for our own good. But none of those terrible storylines are our own. The seeds of most of our fears originated long before we were born. We were fed them, taught them, and gradually made them ours out of loyalty, acceptance, and the need to survive.

Breathing gently with intention—feeling your physical presence while being aware of your surroundings—helps to relieve panic, restore equilibrium, and bring your connection back to reality, in the present.

It takes courage and commitment to unearth painful memories and sufferings and probe for the roots of our fear. In not denying these roots, we begin to recognize what nourished and sustains them. If fear has been your nightmare, releasing it frees the body/mind to finally experience restfulness. It is time to wake up, pull back the covers, turn on the light, and look at what is real in the here and now.

Don't be afraid—if you are afraid, you can't move forward.

·· 10 ··
GRIEF

THE SILENCE OF LOSS CAN BE DEVASTATING and can thrust one into a world outside of time. As the flood gates of grief spill over, a disorienting tidal surge sweeps through, leaving nothing to cling to. For the one who grieves, the past is gone and the future appears to hold no promise. It is a profound letting go into the vastness of an empty now.

Some may want to shrug off the fog of sorrow, call it a bad dream, fill the vacuum with doing, but those denials rob the heart of experiencing and expressing the void. The vulnerability of grief is to be respected, not suppressed out of unpleasantness or shame. Grief takes its own time.

To deny the sanctity of grieving would be to your own or another's detriment. Its mood holds hidden wisdom that is hard won yet profound. Out of this soul-searching hollowness a courageous beauty arises. Flowering all on its own out of the emptiness, it emerges silently, humbly, growing toward the light of renewal.

Grief resides between the worlds of matter and spirit, where the overwhelming pain of loss feels never-ending. Be fully present to those who grieve. Give space, yet be available. Kindness, patience, and compassion prepare the ground for healing.

Shock, pain, and fear are the first stages of grief. Then comes loss and the realization of an unasked-for severing of the bonds of love. We need to pass through the experience of grief with open eyes and an open heart—to cry, to scream, to release the fear. Then, by learning to love and care for ourselves, we can traverse the valleys of depression and hopelessness and begin to heal.

·· 11 ··
SCRUTINY

CONFLICT AND MISUNDERSTANDINGS often result from alternate approaches to the same goal. When diverse perspectives and personalities fail to meet on common ground, patience and respect can help to untangle the knot.

The first step is to take stock of how you have added to the friction: What is your objective? By shifting your focus away from the strife and placing it squarely on yourself, you may find that your aim for a certain result has led you to make assumptions or take others for granted. There might be a déjà vu quality to this time, where it feels as though you've been in this kind of tangle before. Or you may find that, unsuspectingly, you've been on someone else's radar.

Scrutinize any patterns that intentionally or unwittingly have complicated your arrangements. Assigning blame resolves nothing. It simply diverts attention away from your own responsibility. With humility, sincerity, and an open mind, a troublesome situation can change into a respectful one, where every voice is truly heard.

Although this is not a light and breezy time, take it as an overdue reality check. By removing blinders that keep you from seeing the full picture, you can begin straightening out your affairs. It's time to get down, get real, and clean up your act. Become aware of your own or another's manipulative tactics that appear innocent but will create confusing entanglements down the track. When determination is coupled with vigilance and integrity, success is assured.

Insight requires open eyes without rose-colored glasses. A solid foundation cannot be built on the shaky ground of illusions or assumptions.

I have learned that particularly clever ideas do not always stand up under close scrutiny.

·· 12 ··
DETERMINATION

REALIZING A LONG-HELD DREAM requires keeping the fire within alive while learning the self-discipline needed to raise the bar of previous accomplishments. Distinctions are earned, not given. Clarify to yourself the importance of your goal. The amount of time, effort, and dedication required to attain a successful outcome should be worth the cost to *you*, above anyone else, despite the grind of repetitive and demanding routines. A sincere dedication remains on track even when formidable hurdles arise—and they do.

Learning the knack of concentration and focus strengthens the body and mind for tackling a gamut of challenges, especially when facing a long-term commitment.

If every step has begun to feel pointless, consider that your passion may have fizzled, or if your thoughts persist in wandering, it is likely that your mind is searching for motivation elsewhere.

Frustration and disillusionment are hurdles in the process of achievement and have nearly derailed many exemplary accomplishments. To work through low-energy periods, all that may be needed is to reconnect with your sense of purpose that initially lit your inner flame. If you are dragging your heels, making excuses, or playing avoidance games, stop postponing the inevitable. Face that your heart is no longer in it and move on without shaming or blaming anyone, especially yourself. Successes and failures are both needed to achieve excellence the next time around.

Determination is a decision. Day to day, moment to moment, now. It is the capacity to visualize and continue—despite fear, uncertainty, or a shadow that runs with us even as we shine. Determination is a life force that helps you to express your fullest potential.

· 13 ·
PERFECTION

PERFECTIONISTS HOLD HIGH PERSONAL STANDARDS and are often unaware that they can come across as cold, authoritarian, humorless. Their aim to "get it right" is admirable, but habitual faultfinding drains the joy out of life. Playing the role of a classic, nitpicky perfectionist kills all spontaneity and creativity both within and around themselves.

History is packed with stories of powerful men. Rarely are women revered unless as a powerful man's significant other.

Flashback to 1345 BCE when this stunning bust of Egyptian queen Nefertiti was created. To this day, it is considered by many to personify beauty, perfection in human form.

Nefertiti ruled in ancient Egypt alongside her husband, the pharaoh Akhenaten. Together, they created a new religion and proclaimed themselves to be the perfect embodiment of their god. This card acknowledges Nefertiti's authority as queen, and, looking beneath her surface, we see finely tuned gears that must have worked 24/7. After Akhenaten's death, she herself was crowned pharaoh. To command respect, she would have been expected to display all the accoutrements of masculine authority.

Pay attention to any perfectionist tendencies that have unknowingly become self-destructive. Be sure to give yourself and those around you a break from perfectionism's grip by relaxing any tension or frustration you acquired because of it. Once you loosen up and become wonderfully, imperfectly human again, you won't need to prop up a false face—or, for that matter, wear a beard of office!

A break in any perfection lets the light in, offers relaxation. Perfection is an ending—imperfection a beginning. Love the odd, the surprising, the strange in yourself—and then in the world. The temple of beauty permits an open window . . . that's how it breathes.

·· 14 ··
POWER

EOPLE IN POWER often appear larger than life, and some will spare nothing to maintain that image. They will create rules that apply only to themselves and their inner circle, using praise as a trophy while humiliating and marginalizing those they perceive as disloyal. The clear message is that they are to be both respected and feared. Vocal opposition will be ridiculed as naive or condemned as traitorous; active resistance will provoke retribution, regardless of any collateral damage.

Abuse of this kind is present in the boardrooms and bedrooms of today's power brokers and has been for millennia. Whether on the world stage or at home, such manipulative tactics are often used by bullies and bosses. A tyrant always chooses disdain over respect.

Alternatively, the integrity of a genuinely powerful person imparts a compelling, calm authority. Their freedom from self-serving motives illuminates a liberating path, empowering others to stand strong in their own right.

Developing inner authority is the only effective way to deal with those who attempt to impose their power on you. Rather than meeting them on their terms, direct your attention toward strengthening what gives your life meaning and purpose. Even if it requires facing harsh conditions and your own fears, flipping that internal switch will reveal the path toward enlightened self-determination that is unique to you.

There are two powers in the world: one is the sword, and the other is the pen.
There is a third power stronger than both, that of women.

WATER

*Suit of emotions and feelings, relationships,
intuition, flow, art, passion, and harmony,
commonly known as the suit of cups.*

·· 1 ··
FLOW

B E QUIET. LISTEN. And feel the flow of life subtly moving within and around you. You are not the cause of it. It is the stirring energy that, like a watercourse, moves within and throughout everything. It is fluid, lyrical, free—we cannot contain it, but it contains all.

Oppose the flow and life feels antagonistic, threatening our plans and desires that may be driving an exhausting need to force or redirect what's happening for personal gain. It's a defensiveness that strains against the encroaching tide of reality, which always ebbs and flows.

"Going with the flow" is a receptive and attentive attitude that releases preconceptions and enables a conscious partnering with life as it is right now. Living in sync with life's variable rhythms, we learn the art of navigating the current while discovering more about ourselves and the nature of nature in the process. We participate. It's a shared experience that is energizing, inspiring, and beneficial to our overall well-being.

Meditation returns us to the moment, releases us from rehashing the past or stressing about the future. By turning attention inward, we fine-tune the sensitivity that observes impartially, listens attentively, and nourishes the trust that is our inner strength.

Flow is the music of the universe, the essence of life itself. Love creates the trust needed for letting go, flowing with no boundaries, no limits. Then I am totally free to create and to be. I simply float where the current takes me from one note to the next . . . always listening. I am guided deeper into the sounds that invite the next tone, then the next, that gradually flow together into an outpouring of music.

·· 2 ··
UNION

NION IS BORN OUT OF AN ATTRACTION between independent entities. It's a force of nature that makes it possible to conceive and nurture something exceptional.

A marriage of minds needn't compel partners to think the same thoughts or dream the same dreams. No binding contract should obstruct the freedom of anyone in a heartfelt relationship. Partnerships thrive out of mutual respect for the unique qualities of each and from acknowledging individual needs. Allowing spaciousness and independence keeps the atmosphere fresh. When shared ideals are in tune, a rainbow of potential radiates and ripples outward.

The strength of a partnership built on integrity and trust fortifies it to withstand life's surging floods and drifting periods of calm.

Leave your illusions of a perfect union or expectations of an ideal ever-lasting love. These romantic fantasies can only hinder the experience of learning and growing in tandem. When partners support each other through the ever-changing challenges of life, their love becomes a living and bountiful wellspring, the light from which brightens the world.

There are two main spiritual paths—one is the path of love and devotion and the other the path of meditation and witnessing. A person will generally gravitate toward one or the other. Often, feminine energies gravitate toward the path of love, while masculine energies gravitate toward the path of meditation.

When these two meet, this is the path of Tantra. The heights and depths of relationship lived in awareness leads to the absolute nectar of being, a state of inner and outer wholeness. It is everyone's birthright to know and experience union on all levels. It is through union we attain our greatest potential as human beings.

·· 3 ··
HARMONY

SINCE ANCIENT TIMES, dolphins have symbolized happiness, good fortune, and playfulness. As they effortlessly leap from their watery home, they personify the grace and joy of being alive.

Every living thing resonates with a unique vibration or pulse, according to its place in the kingdoms of this world. In varying degrees, the cosmic dance between these vibrations is either harmonious and supportive or out of sync and dissonant.

Respecting the undulating nature of life's flow, and living in harmony with it, is the message here. Listen to your body to learn what it needs to support health and well-being. Seek out the people, conditions, and environments that you naturally resonate with. Learn what makes you feel at ease, valued, and more alive. Increased self-awareness encourages self-confidence that in turn attracts positive experiences and an optimistic outlook.

Breathing in tune with the natural world at daybreak or listening to the "music of the spheres" at night is profoundly healing. It magnifies and fine-tunes our intimate connection with existence while opening the heart and mind in trust to embrace the whole of life. Lighten up, reach out to life, friends, animals, and plants to share your energies, celebrate, and enjoy.

At the center, untouched and free, we are many, we are one, in unconditional love, living in tune with existence. For harmony to emerge from chaos, the balance of male and female principles is needed. The male is structure, discipline; the female is the beauty of floating free. Their harmony is a blissful state that exists in being present in the eternal now in this moment, the next, and the next—and in the silence at the center.

·· 4 ··
FROZEN

WORRY ABOUT THE FUTURE freezes the life out of life. A kind of mental paralysis sets in, where you only see worst-case scenarios—and who in their right mind wants to remain stuck in that?

Disengaging from a standstill requires awareness of how you got stuck—feeling somehow not enough or victimized in the first place. A little self-inquiry is the means for melting an impasse created by self-doubt and dispersing the mindset that constructed it.

What have you been hoping for that hasn't come to pass? Did a buildup of frustration or disappointment cause you to withdraw, give up, or turn your back on opportunities? Giving life the cold shoulder may have been an understandable tactic at one point, but continued frigidity only attracts more frost. Hardening the heart to protect against pain feels safe but comes at the expense of your vitality and enjoyment of life.

Although you may feel shaky and vulnerable, rouse yourself from the tendency to imagine life rather than live it. You dug yourself in, and you have the power to dig yourself out. Detachment does not require that you become an ice queen. Life will be anything but boring once you participate in the flow of opportunities that are already on offer.

Reach out to people and experiences that are interesting, challenging, unusual. Choose to walk on the wild side of the street for a change. Too much self-control may be smothering your spirit.

You have to make mistakes to find out who you aren't. You take the action, and the insight follows.
You don't think your way into becoming yourself.

·· 5 ··
DISAPPOINTMENT

SELF-RECRIMINATION OR FAULTFINDING does nothing to change the pain of disappointment. No joy comes from blaming life, fate, the moon, or yourself, because the root cause lies hidden within emotional contracts that keep you from contentment. Become aware of the ingrained self-defeating habits that undermine your satisfaction and self-worth. Dig deep to unearth old attitudes and beliefs about yourself that continue to trip you up and thereby set the stage for disappointment.

Drop anyone who sucks your energy by denigrating, devaluing, intimidating, or manipulating you. Taking charge of your well-being requires that you be honest with yourself and others regarding who you genuinely feel comfortable with. Empowered self-respect will help put an end to being unfairly treated or believing you're a victim of circumstance.

Emotions are our internal weather. Your emotional barometer will reveal any warming or cooling trends. Like a forecaster anticipating stormy weather, notice when turbulence darkens your horizon. Instead of waiting around for the sun to return, relax into the "nothing is happening yet" gap and prepare for brighter days to come.

It is up to you to bring about what soothes your soul. If you've been hoping for flowers, plant a garden! Decide that you deserve joy, friendship, self-esteem and make the changes necessary to achieve those ends. The longing to finally shake off a cloak of sadness should be tended to with determination that must come from you. You are not a victim, and life owes you nothing. Seize the day—it's yours for the making.

You're wishin' too much, baby. You gotta stop wearing your wishbone where your backbone oughtta be.

⋮⋮ 6 ⋮⋮
PASSION

PASSION IS NEVER NEUTRAL. It either offers unimaginable heights or sucks the life out of you—drains you dry and leaves you searching for more. When a "have it or be had" passion takes over, reason is cast out to sea. Hungry for gratification, desire tosses caution aside and demands satisfaction. At that point of no return, it's impossible to rein it in, let alone stop it.

What role has passion played in your life? How far have you gone to satisfy desire? Would you go there today?

Surfacing from a passionate obsession is disorienting, as though a tidal wave has swept through, leaving debris scattered across what *was* your life. A devastating aftermath can be a wake-up call that demands a total break from someone or something. If it does, salvage what is relevant and let go of the rest.

One day, looking from a cooler perspective, you may appreciate the likely aftermath of all-consuming desire. Awareness of passion's often reckless nature helps distinguish between the compulsive need for gratification versus a surrender that is grounded in trust.

Is there a solo passage through to the realm of moss and dew without these talismans of cooling sweat and soft caresses, the weight of conjoined limbs, the tart and musky smells . . . this breath we share together?

This paradise with you is fleeting, though hours do pass like streetcars in a dream.
But are you the necessary arbiter, the catalyst, the flux, the map, the guide, the honey pot, the candle in the window?

What of a contentment that doesn't fade, a smile that does not falter, a way of being without conditions that sages know and lovers only sample?

·· 7 ··
CHOICES

WHAT IS PUT ON, taken off. Who is the one that chooses it? Watch children playing dress-up—the characters they invent, the creativity they bring to it. Cowboys, queens, witches, and silly clowns, all are welcomed in the game. And unburdened by fixed rules of right or wrong, each child brings their individuality to the role. Innocent authenticity shines through, regardless of the costume worn.

The hats in this image symbolize the characters we create over the course of our lives—changeable, spontaneous. We're free to construct anew, given the circumstances. In India, this play is called *leela*—a philosophical approach that sees everyone, regardless of age or stature, as a child playing at life.

Consider the "hats" you wear while going about the business of being *you*. How many roles do you act out, believing they are real? Which have been with you since childhood, and which do you continue to modify or embellish? Do you have any favorites? Reflect on the roles you've played, your successes and failures according to the situation at the time.

Stop worrying about making mistakes and come back to the one who's wearing the hat. Life is an invitation to experience the merry-go-round world while staying in touch with yourself. It is in this interplay of inner and outer that we come to understand what "know thyself" really means.

And even bone-deep gifts Nature confers—art, music, math—will, if embraced with passion, lead us deeper
to where we find we're equal participants in the whole interconnected festival of life. "Inward" is key.
If we go deep enough, past the sheer singing veil—consciousness lives in a silence like starshine.

·· 8 ··
SEPARATION

UNDER THE DARKENING MOON, a waning connection requires the courage to establish distance. When the fire once shared by two people has gone cold, and communications fail to rekindle that flame, separating can feel like a loss, a negative, a tearing apart. However, it is essential when it arises out of the natural course of cause and effect, growth and change. It opens up time and space for each to reflect upon and reconnect with who they are apart from the relationship.

Separation is an opportunity to discover, or rediscover, the deeper and more essential aspects of who you are. When the "we" dissolves and leaves you alone with the "I," it is time to withdraw from fixating on the other and allow yourself to move separately toward your individual destiny. Life has its timing, and it has brought you to this turning point. Setting personal boundaries is natural, as each must begin to explore who they are without the other.

At this juncture, separation is inevitable and correct. Whether it is an intimate relationship, a business partnership, or a project you've been immersed in, when the energy flow has frozen or become irretrievably altered, growth is impossible.

This card points to the need for space now to come back to yourself. Treat this as an "enough is enough" break. The better acquainted you become with who you are, the less fraught your next steps will be. Take time to realign yourself before creating new connections or obligations. Being on your own now will bring much-needed clarity.

Distance creates another dimension to love—love for oneself.

·· 9 ··
INDULGENCE

ABUNDANCE CAN BE INTOXICATING. When good fortune smiles, the world brightens with opportunity and prosperous conditions seem to attract more prosperity. As the rich get richer, their lives supposedly get easier. They can afford to kick back and worry less about the things that bug everyone else. However, some become stressed and anxious in fear of losing the privilege of abundant good times.

When past worries have vanished and you are replete,

remember to respect your body. Mindlessly feeding whims and desires creates dependence, and that takes diligence to repair.

Success, influence, and satisfaction have tempted this cherub into believing she can have her cake and eat it with abandon. But indulgence without restraint, accumulating without letting go, ultimately tips the scales of fulfilment, which never truly comes from a piece of cake or a shopping spree. And if you believe it's these things that will make you happy, you are deceived. When we ignore our natural limits, the extremes can lead us perilously close to the edge of collapse.

Much has been granted, and if you maintain touch with your center, there is much more to be had! Use this time of plenty to find ways to share. When life is so rich, savor it. Give without conditions and appreciate the bounty while it lasts.

In truth, I am neither the one who eats the cherry first nor the one who saves it for last. When I look back on my experiences of cherries and sundaes, I see that it's always in the middle that I go for the cherry. Like it's the "fulcrum" where diving into the sundae pivots into finishing it off and licking the spoon.

$\cdot\cdot$ 10 $\cdot\cdot$
GRATITUDE

GRATITUDE FROM AN OVERFLOWING HEART is a profoundly personal expression of spirit. It is a humbling state of grace that transcends conventional appreciation and leads us toward the wonder of the ineffable. This intimate experience resonates at a different frequency from the standard paying of respects or expressions of thanks. When pure gratitude flows, it becomes a bridge to the infinite. It is an intimate act, a simple or sublime thanksgiving, devoid of motive or reason.

In this form of gratitude, which some call prayer, time stands still, as the surrounding atmosphere becomes alive, luminous. It's a revelation in which we realize that we are embraced and forever held in love. It holds the power to transform one's life.

Surrender to the upwelling of emotion your gratitude brings—maybe in silence, laughter, or tears. So personal this gift . . . private, sacred, and with no conditions or obligation to write a thank-you note. May gratitude permeate all the days of your life.

Gratitude . . . what comes to mind is my nightly ritual of lying in bed, waiting for sleep. I ask myself, "Are you ready to die?" And when I find the yes, gratitude for life and all its many blessings appears spontaneously. I experience myself as basking in the warm light of thankfulness, in great humility and fragility, giving thanks to the Great Divine Spirit. Nature is my direct connection to an overflowing feeling of gratefulness—that sense of being a small part in the great WHOLE and the awe and wonder that it evokes.

·· 11 ··
IMAGINATION

I N DREAMY INNOCENCE, this young woman visualizes an exciting, free, and colorful future. But the ship of her dreams is without substance. To realize her imagined adventures, she must grow and learn from her not-so-exciting everyday life here and now.

At times, she will have to dig deep to find the fortitude and determination to stay the course. Yet it is through facing disappointments, the indifference of others, or lack of support that she will grow mature and strong. Then, when she is ready, she will finally cast off toward realizing her dream.

Most imaginings remain just that, but they serve a purpose by initiating breakthroughs that help us better understand ourselves and the world we live in. Without imagination there would be no flights to the stars, no way to break through the boundaries of what is already known and acceptable. To bring our imaginings to realization can take moments or years, even a lifetime. But once our dreams take root and ripen, they find a multitude of ways to manifest—in works of art, scientific breakthroughs, leaps of faith, social change . . .

Imagination is an expression of innocence that arises from our inner child. It keeps us young and vital no matter our age.

Sensitivity and patience are called for now; avoid pressuring yourself or someone else to be realistic. And remember that it is impossible to know beforehand what fantasies could one day become miracles.

Imagination is my ability to see the inherent magic permeating all of life—an understanding that I can delight in swimming between the molecules, unencumbered. To look at life without shame and without fearing that what I find will be slapped from my hands.

·· 12 ··
VOYAGER

EVERY LIFE IS A JOURNEY, traveled without map or GPS. We grow as we go, sometimes taking detours, making miscalculations. The meandering river of life is where our skills are honed to increase awareness, gain confidence, and mature.

Our adventure takes place on two concurrent fronts—busy day-to-day affairs in the world and within an inner landscape. In the interior realm, it is an evolving process that develops attention and intention, the practice of living here and now.

This soul journey has no timeline, no arrival, no success or failure. The voyager moves with the current, whether it's calm or turbulent. In time, accepting and assimilating change becomes second nature.

By dropping the desire to control life, we begin to relax into trust and feel supported—guided on the journey. Navigating the unknown increases self-reliance and gratitude for all experiences. If we stay in this openness, panic and fear cannot take root. In truth, we are all voyagers, learning that the art of being fully alive is its own reward.

For thirty-two years, Deva and I have traveled the world. Throughout this voyage we've sailed on the wings of mantra, never spending longer than six months in each place. People ask if I feel homeless— for so long on the road, in different hotel rooms, different cities, countries . . . always moving from somewhere to somewhere. This lifestyle has given the opportunity to consider the difference between feeling homeless or feeling at home wherever I am. We are always at home and happy on this road to now-here. I received a Zen teaching—"there is no goal but the path"—that's the voyage.

·· 13 ··
INTUITION

I NTUITION IS THE PRIMORDIAL KNOWLEDGE of the heart that lives within everyone. This mysterious aspect of human understanding and awareness is transparent. Its elusive divine nature is deeper than the intellect and surpasses it. The "filing cabinet" of the logical mind often fails to recognize the value of enigmatic wisdom that responds to what others miss. Intuition is our perceptive, guiding inner voice.

Intuition drifts within and through us, surfacing spontaneously. Dispensing with boundaries and protocol, it slips effortlessly into difficult and impossible situations, clarifies understanding and restores harmony, then just as suddenly seems to depart. She communicates through the senses, not the intellect. In fact, so-called reasonable minds have long dismissed intuition as "magical thinking," foolishness, even madness. Women, for the most part, have borne the brunt of that scorn. Many have lost their lives for it.

This essentially feminine characteristic is formless and fluid. When her sensitivity is expressed as tears, it should be respected. Her tearfulness enables release while refreshing her spirit. She is a medium who helps decode dreams, moving seamlessly between the conscious realm and the depths of the subconscious. Many artists have partnered with intuition to create timeless, out-of-this-world works that illuminate and speak to the heart.

How does intuition manifest in your life? Do you ignore it when making decisions or relating with others because its unfathomable nature is too mysterious, inexplicable? Intuition is strengthened by paying attention to gut feelings and the heart and noting how they enhance insight into mysterious or confusing conditions. Intuition does not ignore intellect; her inclusive approach unifies with logic and instinct, enabling them to work as one.

Trust your instincts. Intuition doesn't lie.

·· 14 ··
DREAM WEAVER

MEET THE HEARTFUL SAGE of the watery realm of emotions. This poet weaves tales of love and loss from the intersection of dreams and reality. Although he can stretch truth in service of a good story, should his intention be misunderstood, he may take it to heart, become dejected, or withdraw for a time to brood. Later, like sunshine after a storm, the lighthearted companion returns with all hurts forgotten.

Alone time is essential for weavers of dreams and is best spent communing with nature. The natural world is the inspiration and source of his overflowing creativity. When there is a need to refuel the spirit or heal the body, he finds sustenance near the water. He respects children, birdsong, the wind in trees, the feel of a stone washed smooth by time and tides.

Once he commits his heart to anything or anyone, it is lasting. A passion for a philosophy, a cause, or a partner invokes enthusiastic and childlike devotion. A champion of the underdog and a friend to the oppressed, he works tirelessly to serve, whether mending a broken wing, feeding a lost lamb, or tending to the destitute.

Because he displays the strength and fragility of the heart, he can be taken for granted. This is the guy who will give the shirt off his back to anyone in need. You can depend on him for help in a crisis.

He asks that you not overthink your intuition, express compassion toward others, and understand that changes in the natural world play a vital role in your own life. And with a twinkle in his eye, he whispers, "Save room for miracles."

Follow your dreams—they know the way.

A SELECTION OF SPREADS

It will be helpful before using these spreads to refer to the "Working with *The Sacred She*" section in the introduction.

BE HERE NOW

This is a single card for the day. Best to approach it fresh, soon after waking, before you get busy.

Take a moment to clear your mind.

Shuffle the cards, cut the deck three times, reassemble, then spread the cards.

Draw one card and turn it face-up. Take in the images, colors, and card's title and note any feelings or thoughts that first arise. Contemplating the image may reveal all you need; however, reading the text for the card will deepen insight.

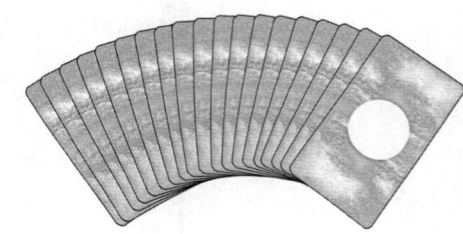

ME AND YOU

This is a two-card spread that addresses your relationship dynamic with a significant other.

Envision yourself summoning insight.

Shuffle the cards, cut the deck three times, reassemble, then spread the cards.

Select one card for yourself. Place it facedown in front of you.

Envision the other person and hold their image in your mind's eye as you draw the second card. Place that card to the right of card 1.

Turn the cards over. Much intuitive insight is contained in your first impression, *before* the rational mind begins formulating and interpreting. Note your feelings, the colors, the card titles, and the first thoughts that arise before you refer to the guidebook for deepening your insight.

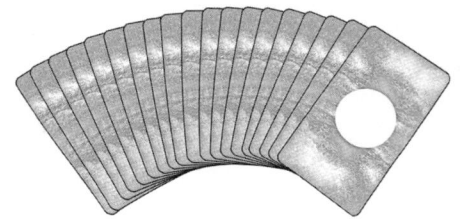

HEAVEN AND EARTH BALANCING HARMONY

This is a three-card spread to reveal the internal and external influences impacting overall harmony or disharmony. This trinity is designed to strengthen self-awareness and your understanding of the impact these influences are having at the present time.

Be still and focus your intention toward gaining insight.

Shuffle the cards. Cut the deck three times, reassemble, and spread the cards facedown.

Select three cards, placing them in the order shown.

Turn the cards faceup in the order they were drawn. Take in the images, colors, and titles and note any feelings that arise upon first impact.

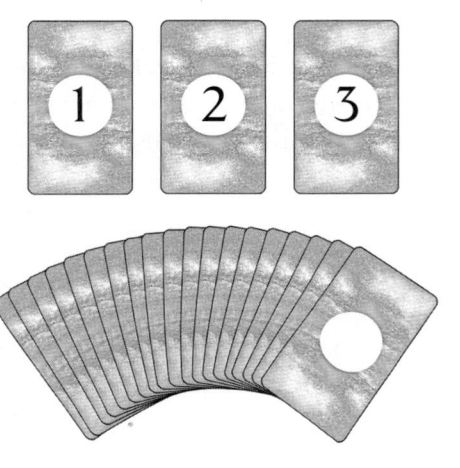

Card 1. This card represents an internal aspect of your psyche that is currently hidden beneath the surface. Bring this attribute into the light of your awareness to understand the basis of your present position.

Card 2. This card represents an external influence impacting your present situation.

Card 3. This is the balancing element. Awareness of this aspect supports restoring equilibrium.

DIAMOND CLARITY

A four-card spread to strengthen trust, clarify areas of uncertainty, and discern a way forward.

Take a moment to center your attention for summoning clarity.

Shuffle the cards. Cut the deck three times, reassemble, then spread the cards.

Select four cards and place them in the order shown. Keep the cards facedown until all four are drawn. Then turn them over in order and contemplate the following questions.

Card 1. What will help me to better understand my issue?

Card 2. What am I unaware of that is either supporting or confusing this issue?

Card 3. What will change once a better understanding is achieved?

Card 4. With the insight gained from cards 1, 2, and 3, what is the way forward?

THE ELEMENTAL STAR OF WELL-BEING

A five-card spread. These five positions designate the basic elements in nature and the body.
The spread reveals influences affecting health and well-being. This insightful reading is best done as a ritual
in a quiet space. Light a candle, perhaps burn incense, and calm your mind.

With eyes closed, invite insight.

Shuffle the cards. Cut the deck three times. Reassemble and spread the deck.

Draw and position each card in the order shown.

Card 1. Spirit/Space: Your connection to spirit, intuition, trust, expansiveness, and realizing potential OR what feeds your self-doubt, disappointment, and fear.

Card 2. Fire: The fire that fuels power, courage, enthusiasm and stimulates inspiration OR what creates exhaustion, is demanding, stressful, or unsupportive.

Card 3. Air: Equilibrium, compulsion, communication. What is supporting clarity and open-mindedness OR what is restricting, limiting, or overshadowing clarity.

Card 4. Water: Adapting, flowing, healing. What helps a relaxed, flowing nature OR what hinders or diverts the flow, creating turbulence.

Card 5. Earth: Foundation and nourishment. What is stabilizing, encouraging confidence and trust OR is what is undermining, discouraging, and creating weakness.

THE SACRED SHE VARIATION
OF THE CELTIC CROSS

The classic Celtic Cross layout is given a new spin. This is a ten-card spread.

Calm your mind while holding the deck. Invite insight.

Shuffle the cards, cut the deck three times, reassemble, then spread the cards.

Draw ten cards, placing them in the order shown. Keep the cards facedown until all ten are drawn. Turn the cards faceup in the same order they were drawn. Take in the images, colors, and card titles and note any emotions or intuition that arises upon first impact.

Card 1. The Present: Your issue.

Card 2. The Challenge: This card is placed diagonally or horizontally across card 1. It is blocking, protecting, or supporting clarity about your issue.

Card 3. What Is Unseen: A subconscious (hidden) influence impacting the issue.

Card 4. A Likely Direction: A development based upon the influences of cards 1 through 3.

Card 5. A Past Pattern: Reveals a habit, root effect, or trigger impacting the situation.

Card 6. The Goal: What you are striving for.

Card 7. Advice: Guidance regarding your present attitude to the issue.

Card 8. Beyond Your Control: External influences that are part of a bigger picture.

Card 9. Your Hopes or Fears: Expectations and doubts regarding the issue.

Card 10. Conclusion: Overview of the inner and outer circumstances taken as a whole.

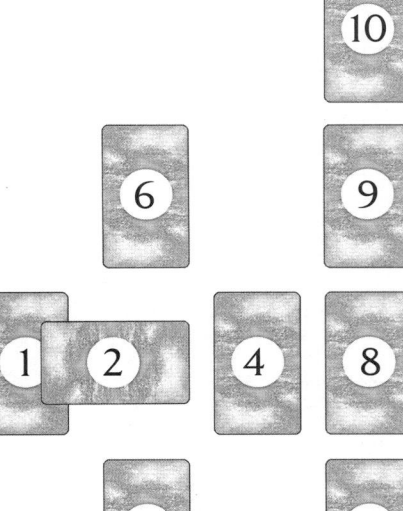

ABOUT THE CREATOR
PADMA, FROM THEN TO NOW

MA DEVA PADMA (Susan Bernard Morgan) was born near Boston, grew up in the suburb of Wellesley, and began drawing as soon as she could hold a crayon. Her innate talents were recognized and encouraged by various art teachers early on.

She attended the New England School of Art and the Boston Museum School of Fine Arts but was impatient to find her own creative path. She married a musician and soon after became a mother.

With baby in tow, she worked as an illustrator for underground newspapers. In 1971 her quest for meaning and greater purpose in life led her to the psychic Gregge Tiffen, whose "life-reading" sessions turned her Harvard Square counterculture existence upside down. For a time, she attended Claudio Naranjo's gestalt therapy sessions. Thanks to Richard Alpert (Ram Dass), she learned of the Buddha's Eightfold Path and sampled different forms of meditation. Drawn to the eclectic mix of consciousness-raising techniques that Oscar Ichazo had merged into his Human Potential Movement, she moved to New York City. There she painted large yantra mandalas, specified by Ichazo for use in his advanced trainings. As her spiritual quest deepened, her attention shifted toward Eastern mysticism.

Along with thousands of seekers, she traveled to India, seeking wisdom from an authentic source. In Mumbai she attended talks by J. Krishnamurti and in 1975 became a disciple of Bhagwan Shree Rajneesh (later called Osho). For many years, Padma considered his commune in India to be her forever home. Shortly before Osho's death, he invited Padma to illustrate his Zen teachings in a set of tarot cards based upon his discourses on Zen Buddhism. Four years later, this work was produced as *Osho Zen Tarot: The Transcendental Game of Zen*, a deck that is enjoyed by millions today.

Padma then left India for New Zealand, where she began a seven-year project devoted to illustrating the Chinese classic *I Ching* as a set of sixty-four oracle cards and accompanying book known as *TAO Oracle: An Illuminated New Approach to the* I Ching, published in 2002. Her decks are considered timeless classics and continue to stand out among the many hundreds of tarot and oracle decks worldwide.

Padma lives and works with her artist husband, Ashika, at their studio in Australia. Her fine art has been exhibited in the United States, Europe, and Asia. She is a prolific painter, art teacher, mentor, and inspiring speaker on incorporating sacred art and tarot into daily practice for deepening self-awareness, furthering meditation, and encouraging well-being.

CONTRIBUTORS, SOURCES & PERMISSIONS

Numerous friends, mentors, and kindred spirits have generously given permission to be quoted in this book. Other quotes were sourced from the works of contemporary luminaries. To learn more about these inspiring and generous souls, please visit www.thesacredshetarot.com.

SPIRIT 0 BEGINNING

Deva Padma. *See* "About the Creator: Padma, from Then to Now."
www.thetaooracle.com, www.embraceart.com

SPIRIT I ALCHEMY

Abhi Ktori-Carter, "Blessed in so many ways by the song and dance of an amazing life, now at seventy-six years I've completed a new music CD, *Bearing Witness.*"
www.essencewave.com

SPIRIT II THE UNKNOWABLE

Turiya Hanover is the cofounder of Path of Love and Working with People trainings. She has integrated Western psychology with Eastern meditation techniques since 1973 and leads trainings around the world.

www.dimensionsofbeing.org,

www. pathreetreats.com,

www.workingwithpeopletrainings.com

SPIRIT III MOTHER NATURE

Catherine Abby Rich has been an herbalist and educator for more than fifty years and is an Ampcoil Ambassador and quantum SCIO practitioner. "My best medicine is 'A Remedy for These Times.'"

SPIRIT IV ORDER

Sidd Murray-Clark is an internationally exhibited artist and founder of Creative Vision for Life. He is an author, illustrator, and graphic artist. Sidd leads meditation-based creativity workshops in the European Union and Japan.

www.siddart.com

SPIRIT V WISDOM KEEPER

Voge Smith is the award-winning author of *I Release! Create the Life That Makes Your Heart Sing*, as well as a mentor, trauma alchemist, and therapist for the past thirty-five years.

www.vogesmith.com

SPIRIT VI LOVE

St. Teresa of Avila, *The Collected Works of St. Teresa of Avila, Vol. 2*, trans. Kieran Kavanaugh and Otilio Rodriguez (Washington, DC: ICS Publications, 1980), 434.

Spirit VII Turning Point
Rupda, SE, NVC, NLP, HC, is an SIAF counselor, and she teaches authentic leadership and self-development. Rupda's unique Leadership Rupbellion supports individuals, groups, and organizations worldwide.
www.rupda.com

Spirit VIII Compassion
Tony Kendrew, MA (creative writing, University of Wales), is a poet and author. Tony's titles include *Feathers Scattered in the Wind*, *Turning*, and a collection of short stories, *Tranatlanecdotes*.
www.tonykendrew.com

Spirit IX Solitude
Rashid Maxwell, a biographer and designer of buildings and landscapes for sacred use, is a lover of the arts and everything else.
www.rashidmaxwell.com

Spirit X Change
Priya Huffman, MA, formerly a Jungian psychotherapist, is a sucker for beauty and in awe of the creativity of ordinary life.
www.priyahuffman.com

Spirit XI Balancing
Bhadrena C. Tschumi, MA, BCST, RCST, PPNP, SEP, eidg. dipl., KT, has lectured on the biodynamic approach to craniosacral therapy for forty years, teaching therapists to recognize health in each manifestation of body-mind-spirit.
www.icsb.ch

Spirit XII Waking Up
Sudhir Dean, BA (social science), focuses on trauma from abuse in his work. He is also a musician, interna-

tionally known astrology columnist, and author of *Astrology for Those Who Won't Admit They're Interested*.
www.sudhircounselling.com

SPIRIT XIII TRANSITIONING
Prakash Mackay, MA (psychology and drama), has worked for thirty-six years with Hospice Maui as a spiritual care coordinator and bereavement counselor. He reads tarot, is a calligrapher, holds a black belt in Aikido, and teaches Diamond Approach at Ridhwan School in the US and UK.
www.facebook.com/prakashmackay

SPIRIT XIV KARMA
Adrienne Hall is a lifelong traveler and explorer of cultures and philosophies. "I love people, nature, wildlife, music, poetry, and our beautiful planet. I am forever grateful!"

SPIRIT XV REPRESSION
Avikal E. Costantino, "You could call me a mystic." He helps people discover their unique spirit and integrate it into their life. He leads workshops and retreats globally. His most recent title is *Who Is In? Beyond Self-image*.
www.integralbeing.com, www.avikal.co

SPIRIT XVI CRISIS
Premrup Streiker, BA, MEd, MSW, PhD, is listed in *Feminists Who Changed America (1963–1975)*. A playwright of *A Waltz for Women's Voices*, she's a radical feminist, therapist, mother of three, and grandmother of four.

SPIRIT XVII UNDERSTANDING
Visarjan Barker, "My life is rich in creativity and service to others. The work of artists and artisans in all their forms is my passion."
www.eurekaantiques.com.au

Spirit XVIII Anxiety

Benjamin Stott, DAOM, LAc, is the cofounder of Three Harmonies Acupuncture with more than thirty years experience. He studied in China and is also a martial artist, meditator, and poet. "My life isn't a project anymore, just oh so much to respond to and celebrate."

Spirit XIX Joy

Prartho Sereno is a counseling psychologist, mother of two, meditation instructor at Cornell University, book and cover illustrator, prize winning poet, and Poet Laureate of Marin County, California. Prartho teaches the Poetic Pilgrimage online.
www.prarthosereno.com

Spirit XX Liberation

Turiya Hanover. *See* Spirit II The Unknowable.

Spirit XXI Wisdom

Bernadette Noll, "I Want to Age Like Sea Glass," *Huffington Post* (blog), May 14, 2014, https://www.huffpost.com/entry/i-want-to-age-like-sea-glass_b_5317199. Copyright © 2014 by Bernadette Noll. Excerpt used with permission. She is the author of *Slow Family Living* and two other titles.
www.bernadettenoll.net

Earth 1 Roots

Tony Kendrew. *See* Spirit VIII Compassion.

Earth 2 Be Here Now

Margery Cantor currently runs the Impermanent Press in Norwich, Vermont, with Luna, her beloved Labrador retriever. Margery has designed books for Scribner, Knopf, Shambhala, HarperSanFrancisco, and many more.

Earth 3 Cooperation

Santoshi Stone is an entrepreneur and health and wellness practitioner. She uplifts and guides others to reach their full potential and turn their dreams into reality. www.sharesuccess.com.au, www.mydoterra.com /adheeshandsantoshi

Earth 4 Consuming

Elizabeth Gilbert, *Big Magic: Creative Living Beyond Fear* (New York: Riverhead Books, 2015), 171.

Earth 5 Perseverance

Ashika graduated from Emily Carr Institute of Art. A martial artist, illustrator, and retired stone sculptor, he lives with his wife, Padma, at their bushland studio in Australia. www.embraceart.com, www.thespiritjourney.net

Earth 6 Generosity

Premda Haberle is a writer/rancher who lives in the foothills of the Sierra Nevada mountains. At the Hoffman Institute, she developed a method to interpret emotional history through body language.

Earth 7 Timing

Komala Kuroda, "I support the love and joy of living and creating the life you love." Komala is an essential life consultant and heart meditation teacher from Unity Institute and an Aura-Soma® practitioner. www.puskara.jp

Earth 8 Labor of Love

Parmita Pushman is a record-label founder and artisan. She cofounded White Swan Records with a catalog of music for yoga and meditation. www.prajnaparamitamalas.com, www.whiteswanrecords.com

EARTH 9 SATISFACTION
Priya Huffman. *See* Spirit X Change.

EARTH 10 PRIVILEGE
Priya Huffman. *See* Spirit X Change.

EARTH 11 HONESTY
Premda Haberle. *See* Earth 6 Generosity.

EARTH 12 EXPLORE
Vicki Weissler Horn is a doctor of oriental medicine, acupuncturist, and homeopath. "Mine has been a lifetime of healing, inquiring, loving, dancing, celebrating."
www.drvickiweissler.com

EARTH 13 SUPPORT
Deanne Kallman, BA (art), ECE, is a TAT professional, Reiki practitioner, retired teacher, artist, writer, and elder care companion. She is the founder of Healing Portal of Grace.
www.facebook.com/healingportalofgrace

EARTH 14 RESPECT
Eva Wells, "I'm a grandmother, artist, and earth lover who loves having my hands in the soil. Ceramic clay shows me the way to its creation for my bowls and figurative sculptures."
www.facebook.com/byevajivanwells,
www.facebook.com/MotherEarthSkirts

FIRE 1 INSPIRATION
Simon Dow is a director, choreographer, and master teacher of the Australian Ballet School. Formerly with the Stuttgart, San Francisco, Boston, and Washington Ballets, he now finds expression in photography.
www.simondowphotographer.com

Fire 2 Focus

Nancy Owen Barton, BS (dance history and performance), is a literary agent, editor, and contributor to works that inspire readers and better the world, including *The Sacred She Tarot*, *The Illuminated Hafiz*, *The Purity of Desire*, *Darling I Love You!*, and *On Being Different*.
www.nobaliterary.com

Fire 3 Refresh

Deva Dwabha, MA (psychology UCLA), is the creator and director of Ramana's Garden Children's Home. "I am passionate about kids, education, creative arts, animals, and nature."
www.ramanas.org

Fire 4 Dance

Tika Morgan is a professional dancer, choreographer, and teacher devoted to dance as a way of life by expressing historical and symbolic dance forms to "dance our human story." Her methodology is both reverent and joyous.
www.tikamorgandance.com

Fire 5 Competition

Sandhan Johnson is a leader of online multidimensional wealth creation, supporting people to step into a world of possibility and abundance.
www.facebook.com/sandhaninc

Fire 6 Triumph

Pankaja Brooke, BA (honorary, London Film School), is an internationally acclaimed documentary filmmaker who published novels under the name Dinah Brooke in the 1970s, one of which was republished in 2023 by McNally Editions.
www.pankajabrooke.com

Fire 7 Adaptability
Richard J. Bochniak, BA (theater arts), "Looking for all those banana peels of life to slip on."
www.richcomedian.com

Fire 8 Self-Confidence
Tarika C. Glubin, MA (psychology), "Freedom from the past means a life of presence, love, and responsibility." For more than forty years, she has supported people all over the world to discover their being.
www.free4being.com, www.transessencetechnique.com

Fire 9 Resistance
Ashika. *See* Earth 5 Perseverance.

Fire 10 Overload
Jamila White, "Sis, the inability to receive support from others is a trauma response," Facebook, September 15, 2020, https://www.facebook.com/InspiredJamila/photos/a.543152759084556/3498211960245273.

Fire 11 Self-Expression
Peggy Sands is an artist, designer, and illustrator at Indigo Disegno. She is a Rhode Island School of Design graduate and teaches "Drawing Without Fear." She is art director of the Sedona Winefest and Direct Source Wealth.
www.peggysands.com

Fire 12 Intention
Vicki Weissler Horn. *See* Earth 12 Explore.

Fire 13 Spontaneity
Parmita Pushman. *See* Earth 8 Labor of Love.

FIRE 14 INTEGRITY
Amanda Gorman, "Using Your Voice Is a Political Choice," filmed November 2018 in New York, NY, TED video, 1:44–1:50, https://www.ted.com/talks/amanda _gorman_using_your_voice_is_a_political_choice.

AIR 1 CLARITY
Sandy Gordon, "I am a student of beauty who is devoted to creating and supporting all forms of life in our sacred world. I help people make order out of chaos."

AIR 2 RESTRAINT
Elizabeth Gilbert, *Big Magic: Creative Living Beyond Fear* (New York: Riverhead Books, 2015), 149.

AIR 3 HEARTBREAK
Sidd Murray-Clark. *See* Spirit IV Order.

AIR 4 REST
Vidya Heisel is a master yoga teacher trainer at Frog Lotus Yoga International. She teaches exclusively at her beautiful Suryalila Retreat Centre in Andalusia, Spain. www.suryalila.com

AIR 5 ARROGANCE
Laura Teresa Marquez, FinestQuotes.com, accessed November 25, 2022, http://www.finestquotes.com/quote -id-31582.htm.

AIR 6 DEPARTURE
Komala Kuroda. *See* Earth 7 Timing.

AIR 7 DECEPTION
Lily Dunn is an author, mentor, lecturer, and teacher. She co-runs London Lit Lab at Bath Spa University. Her

book *Sins of My Father: A Daughter, a Cult, a Wild Unravelling* has been met with critical acclaim.
www.lilydunn.co.uk

Air 8 Blame
Avikal E. Costantino. *See* Spirit XV Repression.

Air 9 Fear
Malala Yousafzai, *I Am Malala: The Girl Who Stood Up for Education and Was Shot by the Taliban* (New York: Little, Brown and Company, 2013), 308.

Air 10 Grief
Philip Lake, Samudro, has a diploma in counseling from Oxford College, UK. Philip leads grief therapy seminars. "We are not divided by nationality. In meditation we are one."
www.samudroprem.com

Air 11 Scrutiny
Elizabeth Peters, *The Hippopotamus Pool* (New York: Warner Books, 1996), 329.

Air 12 Determination
Tika Morgan. *See* Fire 4 Dance.

Air 13 Perfection
Madhuri Z K Akin is a poet, memoirist, intuitive reader, and artist who loves walking about and travel. She is the author of multiple titles, including *Mistakes on the Path* and *The Teenage Poems and What I've Learned Since, Vols. 1 and 2*.
www.madhurijewel.com

Air 14 Power
Malala Yousafzai, *I Am Malala*, 31.

WATER 1 FLOW
Deuter helped define the genre of New Age music. In 1985, with New Earth Records, his renown as a New Age musician spread worldwide. "For me, creating music is like painting with sound."
www.newearthrecords.com/artists/music-by-deuter

WATER 2 UNION
Ananda Sarita is a tantra master, mystic, author, and international leader of tantra groups for positive transformation.
www.anandasarita.com, www.tantra-essence.com

WATER 3 HARMONY
Sandipa is inspired by the earth. Her paintings are expressions of the wonder of nature.
www.sandipa.com.au

Sambodhi Prem, a musician with many albums, lives with Sandipa in Australia, where the native birds inspire him.
www.sambodhiprem.com

WATER 4 FROZEN
Anne Lamott, "Becoming the Person You Were Meant to Be: Where to Start," *O, The Oprah Magazine*, November 2009, https://www.oprah.com/spirit/how-to-find-out-who-you-really-are-by-anne-lamott/all.

WATER 5 DISAPPOINTMENT
Elizabeth Gilbert, *Eat, Pray, Love* (New York: Viking, 2006), 150.

WATER 6 PASSION
Benjamin Stott. *See* Spirit XVIII Anxiety.

WATER 7 CHOICES
Madhuri Z K Akin. *See* Air 13 Perfection.

WATER 8 SEPARATION
Madhuri Z K Akin. *See* Air 13 Perfection.

WATER 9 INDULGENCE
Carol Neiman uses words to express the inexpressible and has collaborated with Padma on *Osho Zen Tarot*, the *TAO Oracle*, and now *The Sacred She Tarot*.

WATER 10 GRATITUDE
Deva Premal is a Grammy-nominated musician who, with her partner in life and music, Miten, has toured internationally since 1992 and sold more than a million albums under their record label Prabhu Music.
www.devapremalmiten.com

WATER 11 IMAGINATION
Upasana Evangelia Artemis Papadopoulos, BPsych, MA (curating), works at museums in Naarm and Melbourne.
www.instagram.com/earthlili

WATER 12 VOYAGER
Miten tours the world with his life partner, Deva Premal. Their sacred music and mantra chanting has a fanbase that includes Cher, the Dalai Lama, Tony Robbins, Eckhart Tolle, and millions more.
www.devapremalmiten.com

WATER 13 INTUITION
Oprah Winfrey, "The Top 20 Things Oprah Knows for Sure," Oprah.com, accessed November 25, 2022, https://www.oprah.com/spirit/the-top-20-things-oprah-knows-for-sure.

WATER 14 DREAM WEAVER
Kobi Yamada is president/CEO at Compendium and the *New York Times* bestselling author of *What Do You Do with an Idea?*
www.live-inspired.com

GLOSSARY OF SYMBOLISM

Air element—communication, thought, impulse

Air element in the body—breath, nervous system, movement (*see* five elements)

alligator/crocodile—primordial, fearsome messenger from the subconscious

archer—visionary, far-seeing

arrow—sustaining, life, power, alliance

baby—birth, innocence, potential, vulnerability, purity

bamboo—giving, flexible, yielding

bat—rebirth, of two worlds, seeing beyond the known

bee—sustaining life, devotion, protector, teamwork, industrious, messenger

bird—freedom, imagination, possibilities, happiness

blade—vengeance, cutting through, dividing, freeing

bow—power, vision, accuracy

branch (broken)—letting go of the old, fundamental change

brick/stone wall—rigid, unmovable, stuck, blocking, defending

butterfly—transformation, lightness, temporariness, fragility

candle—guidance, metaphor for soul, enlightenment

cat—mystery and magic, elegance, curiosity, spirituality

chandelier—holder or magnifier of light

child—wonder, freshness, alive, open, innocence, play

circle—void, spirit, wholeness, no beginning no end, emptiness

clouds—mind, thoughts, ever-changing nature

cockatoo—commitment, unfettered self-expression, playfulness, mischief

cow—motherhood, generosity, fertility, nurturing, Gaia, earth medicine

coyote—unpredictable, clever, trickster

crab—fearless, defensive, protection

crow—a messenger, intelligence, psychic ability, teamwork

crystal—insight, clarity, transparency

cup—open, receptive, ritual, ceremony, the heart

dagger—sacrifice, betrayal, cutting through, separating

diamond—many facets, reflection, eternity, enduring

dog—loyalty, protection, family

dolphin—playfulness, intelligence, sensitivity, delight

dragonfly—change, transformation, dreaming, illusion

eagle—inspiration, strength, authority, spirituality, bridge between heaven and earth

Earth—our planetary home, mother nature, grounding, calming, rooted, solid

Earth element in the body—bones, teeth, nails, muscles, connecting tissues, hair and skin (*see* five elements)

egg—potential, womb, fragility, simplicity

Ether—spaciousness, the void or formless container of all existence

Eye of Horus—protection, well-being, wholeness

eyes, closed—looking inward, meditation, sleep

eyes, open—awareness, awake, shocked

falcon—swiftness, purpose, mental agility, vigilance, leadership

feather—trust, honor, achievement, the presence of spirit

Fire—life force, dynamic energy, strength, inspiration, passion

Fire element in the body—metabolism; burns toxins and impurities; drives hunger, thirst, and sleep (*see* five elements)

five elements—earth, air, fire, water, space; a simplified breakdown of the complexity of nature and the interrelationship of each element within the human body

flowers—fulfilled potential, innocence

fox—clever, seductive, adaptable

frog—peace, fertility, rejuvenation, regeneration, strength out of weakness

gate, closed—barrier, fear, suspicion, defensive

gate, open—passage, portal, transition

gears—precision, perfection, control, passing of time

gold—sun, masculine, wealth, truth

hand, clenched—threat, aggression, power, resistance

hand, open—receptive, giving, expression, protection, divine power, blessing

hands, raised upward—adoration, worship, prayer, receptivity, wonder

heart—center of emotion, tenderness, affection, love, romance

horse—courage, freedom, power, valor

howling—warning, group solidarity, connection to the wild

infinity symbol—eternity, limitless, timeless, returning

ivy—peace, immortality, commitment, loyalty, clinging

jasmine flower—grace, elegance, sweetness

kangaroo—stamina, boundless energy, transitioning

key—unlocking hidden meanings of things, knowledge, message from beyond, sign from the spirit guides

kite—youth, play, independence

koala—innocence, affection, love, feminine energy

lamb—purity, humility, gentleness, innocence, a peaceful nature

leaves—nature, maturity, fullness of life, letting go

leopard—agility, self-reliance, rare beauty, intelligence, speed

lightning—shock, abrupt change, illumination or destruction

lion—majesty, courage, strength, confidence, justice

lizard—regeneration, patience, good luck, protection

lotus flower—rebirth, resilience, transformation, enlightenment, purity

mandala—a symbolic diagram denoting spirit, existence, the cosmic drama, and the soul's journey toward a center of unity and oneness, created for contemplation and meditation

Metatron's cube—symbolizing the underlying patterns of the universe connecting the earth with the divine

moon—feminine symbol, the passage of time, immortality, mystery

mountain—permanence, centered, stillness, spiritual elevation, overview

mouth—consuming, greedy, devouring, astonishment

night—secrets, intuition, dreaming, death, rest

owl—wisdom, intuition, observant, silent watcher, supernatural power

pentacle/pentagram—a five-pointed star, contained within a circle; each of the star's five points represent an element (*see* five elements); in many tarot decks, pentacles denote an earthy suit associated with security, stability, wealth; sometimes referred to as the suit of coins or discs in various tarot decks

phoenix—transformation, resurrection, rebirth

poppy—imagination, regeneration, eternal life of the soul, remembrance

rainbow—hope, good fortune, new beginnings, beauty of spirit in everything

red carpet—symbol of being special, elevated privilege, reserved for gods

ribbons—freedom of expression, spontaneity, connection

rock—strength, durability, steadiness

robe—seeking truth, spirituality, healing, humility, liberation

roots—stability, strength, ancestry, history

rope—security, bondage, betrayal, restricted, withholding, tied down

rose—love, happiness, spiritual awakening, balance, beauty

sea—unfathomable depth, chaos, power, mystery, inner feelings, vastness

seahorse—good luck, healing, gentleness, prosperity, emotional clarity

shell—eternity, protection, awareness, sound, purity, mystic spiral

Shri Yantra—representing the source of all power, the divine mother (*see* star, six-pointed)

skull—mortality, wisdom, strength, finality, death

snow—winter, purity, cold, sadness, frozen feelings, hibernation

snowflake—fragility, impermanence

space—origin, omnipresent, container of all the elements, inner wisdom determines hopes and fears (*see* five elements)

spider—connection, perseverance, feminine power, creator, ancient wisdom

spiderweb—beauty, creativity, strength, fragility, destiny, fate

star, five-pointed—light, spiritual, instruction, direction (*see* pentacle)

star, six-pointed—comprised of upward and downward pointing triangles, i.e., masculine and feminine triangles representing creation, the Seal of Solomon

star, seven-pointed—the Great Mother, the macrocosm, wonder, totality, transcending time

star, eight-pointed—completion, regeneration, wholeness, solidarity

stars—forever, destiny, hope, faith, divinity, spirit, the eyes of night

sun—clarity, power, masculine, strength, spirit, divine assistance

sunflower—joy, loyalty, fertility, generosity, optimism

swan—beauty, grace, loyalty

tear—release, realization of truth, acceptance, grief, letting go

thunder—honesty, power, breaking through

tiger—strength, fearlessness, determination, independence

tortoise—the beginning of creation, Earth, longevity, fertility, strength, endurance

tree—dynamic life force, growth, prosperity, rootedness, feminine power of nourishment and regeneration, sheltering, wisdom

veil—mystery, the unknown, hidden, secret, divinely recognized authority

Water—wisdom, power, music, flowing, life, circulation, transformation

Water element—flow, adaptability, purifying, nourishing

Water element in the body—regulates blood and bodily fluids (*see* five elements)

wheat—fertility, bounty, resurrection, abundance

wind—freedom, transient, spirit, change

wings—freedom, message from gods, purity, spirituality

winter—introspection, personal struggle, death and rebirth, ending, detachment

wolf—loyalty, family, teamwork, freedom, guardian, instinct, playfulness

yantra—a mystical diagram used for contemplation, meditation, and worship

yin/yang—duality, the interconnected and complementary oppositional forces of all in existence, female/male, balance, order

SPLENDID BOOKS

Every one of these books is a joy.

Astrology for the Soul by Jan Spiller (Bantam Books, 1997)

Circe by Madeline Miller (Little, Brown and Company, 2018)

Crazy Brave: A Memoir by Jo Harjo (W. W. Norton & Company, 2012)

The Dance of the Dissident Daughter by Sue Monk Kidd (HarperCollins Publishers, 1996)

The Enneagram: Understanding Yourself and the Others in Your Life by Helen Palmer (HarperCollins Publishers, 1988)

The Faithful Gardner: A Wise Tale About That Which Can Never Die by Clarissa Pinkola Estés, PhD (HarperCollins, 1995)

Feeding Your Demons: Ancient Wisdom for Resolving Inner Conflict by Lama Tsultrim Allione (Little, Brown Spark, 2008)

Goddesses in Everywoman: Powerful Archetypes in Women's Lives by Jean Shinoda Bolen, MD (HarperCollins Publishers, 1985)

Letter to My Daughter by Maya Angelou (Random House, 2008)

Mistakes on the Path by Madhuri (M J Press, 2019)

Refuge: An Unnatural History of Family and Place by Terry Tempest Williams (Vintage Books, 1992)

Sacred Contracts: Awakening Your Divine Potential by Caroline Myss (Three Rivers Press, 2002)

Seventy-Eight Degrees of Wisdom: A Book of Tarot by Rachel Pollack (HarperCollins Publishers, 1980)

Sins of My Father: A Daughter, a Cult, a Wild Unravelling by Lily Dunn (Orion Publishing Co., 2022)

Slow Family Living: 75 Simple Ways to Slow Down, Connect, and Create More Joy by Bernadette Noll (TarcherPerigee, 2013)

Start Where You Are: A Guide to Compassionate Living by Pema Chödrön (Shambhala, 2018)

When God Was a Woman by Merlin Stone (Mariner Books, 1978)

When Things Fall Apart: Heart Advice for Difficult Times by Pema Chödrön (Shambhala, 1997)

When Women Were Birds: Fifty-Four Variations on Voice by Terry Tempest Williams (Picador, 2013)

Who Cooked the Last Supper: The Women's History of the World by Rosalind Miles (Three Rivers Press, 2001)

Wisdom Rising: Journey into the Mandala of the Empowered Feminine by Lama Tsultrim Allione (Enliven Books, 2018)

The Woman's Encyclopedia of Myths and Secrets by Barbara G. Walker (HarperCollins, 1983)

Women Who Run with the Wolves: Myths and Stories of the Wild Woman Archetype by Clarissa Pinkola Estés, PhD (Ballantine Books, 1996)